REIMAGINING
FIRE

THE FUTURE OF ENERGY

REIMAGINING FIRE

THE FUTURE OF ENERGY

Edited by Eveline Kolijn

Foreword by Chris Turner

DURVILE &
UpRoute Books

UPROUTE IMPRINT OF DURVILE & UPROUTE BOOKS
CALGARY, ALBERTA, CANADA
DURVILE.COM

Durvile Publications Ltd.

UPROUTE IMPRINT OF DURVILE AND UPROUTE BOOKS

Calgary, Alberta, Canada
www.durvile.com

LIBRARY AND ARCHIVES CATALOGUING IN PUBLICATIONS DATA

Reimagining Fire: The Future of Energy
Kolijn, Eveline: Editor
Turner, Chris: Foreword

1. Environment | 2. Natural Resources | 3. Conservation | 4. Ecosystems
| 5. Canadian Art | 6. Energy Transition

The UpRoute Every River Lit Series | Series Editor, Lorene Shyba

ISBN: 978-1-990735-13-4 (print pbk) | ISBN: 978-1-990735-39-4 (ebook)
ISBN: 978-1-990735-40-0 (audio)

Jacket design: Nadia Perna | Book design: Lorene Shyba and Eveline Kolijn
Typeset in Ubuntu, Scala, and Scala Sans

We acknowledge the traditional land of the Treaty 7 Peoples of Southern Alberta: the Siksika, Piikani, and Kainai of the Niisitapi (Blackfoot) Confederacy; the Dene Tsuut'ina; and the Chiniki, Bearspaw, and Wesley Stoney Nakoda First Nations. Also the Region 3 Métis Nation of Alberta.
We also wish to acknowledge all First Nations, Métis and Inuit persons residing away from their traditional communities, but whom still live in Alberta.

Durvile Publications gratefully acknowledges the financial support of The Government of Canada through Canadian Heritage Canada Book Fund and The Government of Alberta, Alberta Media Fund. Eveline Kolijn would like to thank Calgary Arts Development.

Printed and bound in Canada by Friesens. First Printing. 2023.
All rights reserved. Contact Durvile Publications Ltd. for details.

To Henrik and Amelia, they are the future.

CONTENTS

Transition Prisms, Eveline Kolijn. Etchings, constructed into prisms.
Artist's statement is at the end of Chapter 16.

FOREWORD

Chris Turner

A LL THE BASIC NECESSITIES of life revolve around energy. Acquiring it, harnessing it, using it to cook food or boil water or warm a dwelling against the cold. Fire is the original energy source, the first one that human populations could control, distribute, increase or decrease as needed. And fire remains central to the production of energy, and to the metaphorical lens we use to understand our relationship with energy.

Most of the world's transport is driven by contained explosions— passenger jets soaring across oceans do so on ribbons of fire, and so does the family car for most of us—and much of the world's electricity is produced by boiling water through one method or another to spin turbines, a sort of refinement on fire's ancient role in our lives. Fire, in many senses, remains our primary energy source.

Fire is also the engine of the stories we tell. Stories are a kind of food—the soul's most vital food, I'd wager, after love—and we first fed each other in this way, gathered around campfires, huddled against the night, its cold and its cloaked dangers, telling stories to explain our place on the land and in the universe. Telling stories to explain what makes us human, what makes us families and clans and tribes. Fires on the savannah, fires in a simple home's hearth, fires in the furnaces of generations of homes, the fires in the electronic hearth of the TV or computer screen. What makes us human—what makes us singularly so, what unites us as a species apart from all the others—more than our quest for fire and our insatiable need to share our stories, gathered in one sense or another around a fire?

Fire comes at a cost. We've only just begun to tally up how great that cost truly is, but we have discovered with grim certainty that fire's life-giving and life-fulfilling gifts have come at a dire price. The burning of fires in the industrial age—the big ones, the furnaces of industrial scale and power, fuelled mainly by oil and coal and natural gas—have amassed into an existential threat to humanity's very survival. "The fires have leapt from their furnaces"—this is how Richard Harrison puts it in his poem "And It Bursts With Light," one of many bracing pieces that wrestle with our complicated relationship with fire and its proxies in the pages that follow. The climate crisis, born of two blazing centuries, is now upon us. Some scientists—the ones tasked with naming and defining geological time—suggest this is in fact a new epoch, wrought by human hands. Wrought, more precisely, by the monumental fires human hands have lit and fed. They call it the Anthropocene—the time made by Anthropos, by people. It might just as well be called the Pyrocene, the time made by fire.

The vital task of this troubling new epoch is to radically reconfigure our relationship with energy—with fire and everything else. Energy transitions of such magnitude have historically happened across centuries, even millennia, as human societies have slowly developed and adapted to new technologies based on new energy sources. This time, we are transitioning deliberately, as fast as possible, to a global energy system that is free of the greenhouse gas emissions driving the climate crisis—a global energy system free of fire, or at least free of fire's choking smoke. Over the past two decades, as the scope of the climate crisis has become clear, a toolkit has been hastily assembled to accomplish this task. (It might not seem so hasty, not as the daily news fills with reports of disaster, but we are in fact moving very, very fast.) But human societies do not make these transitions on the strength of tools alone—especially not at the speed the crisis obliges.

We need stories by the fire—essays, poems, art, fiction, all of it—to help guide and inspire us. There is a line widely attributed to Antoine de Saint-Exupéry that goes like this: "If you want to build a ship, don't drum up the men to gather wood, divide the work and give orders. Instead, teach them to yearn for the vast and endless sea." Like so many quotes these days that become memes, it appears not to come directly from the French author's work—it's a paraphrase, refined into a kind of slogan. But it's no less worthwhile for the uncertainty of its origins. It speaks to a deep truth—we are not persuaded to dramatic action or substantial change or great works of collective resolve by our tools, nor by their technical details. Not by the data they generate, not by the concentration of carbon dioxide in parts per million graphed in an accusatory line gone almost straight upward, not even by the cost per kilowatt-hour of solar power in a line gone nearly identically straight downward. Numbers don't move us to yearning for vast seas. Stories do.

The energy transition now underway needs more stories. We need narratives of escape, survival, salvage, even (maybe especially) triumph. Some of these narratives are gathered here. Many more have yet to be written, painted, sculpted.

I've spent twenty years charting the first searching chapters of this energy transition, and I've been convinced beyond doubt it is, at its core, an optimistic tale. It is perilous but thrilling, a story not of mere survival but of great opportunity. It is about building a better world. If we succeed—and I believe we will, even though there will be great loss still to come along the path—it will be a story of collaboration and cooperation on a scale and with a speed never before seen in human history. And it is already underway, and it is accelerating. We have already begun to reimagine fire.

Chris Turner, foreword writer, is an award-winning author and one of Canada's leading writers and speakers on climate change solutions and the global energy transition. His latest book is How To Be A Climate Optimist, *a survey of the first two decades of progress on solving the climate crisis. His previous books on climate, energy and technology include* The Patch *(winner of the National Business Book Award),* The Leap *and* The Geography of Hope, *and his essay and feature writing have received* 10 National Magazine Awards.

Mendeleyev's Dream, Mary Kavanagh. Photograph (Sky detail);
watercolour on paper (Periodic Table of the Elements).
Artist's statement is at the end of Chapter 6.

INTRODUCTION

Eveline Kolijn

Origins: Fire and the Sun

FIRE IS AN ELEMENTAL POWER. It burns and destroys, but also protects and nurtures. Fire was our first source of energy and has fueled many inventions. Anthropologist Lévi-Strauss postulated that fire is the foundation of human culture—the difference between the raw and the cooked. Firelight enabled prehistoric humans to create their first marks and images on the walls of deep dark caves, the origins of the images and stories that contain the power to transmit knowledge and culture over space and time. A Greek myth tells us that fire is a gift to humanity from the titan Prometheus, who in some stories was also our creator, forming the first people out of clay. Things made of clay need to be touched by fire to keep their shape, but fire cannot ignite without something to burn, and for millions of years, that something was plant life, wood.

Trees came into being because 3.5 billion years ago, early cyanobacteria harnessed sunlight to turn water and carbon dioxide into oxygen and the sugars they needed for food. This revolutionary process, called photosynthesis, created the possibility for these microscopic single-celled algae to be absorbed into plants as chloroplasts and evolve into larger and more numerous plant species. With their emergence, plants were able to sustain animal life, so ultimately, almost all life on our planet is powered by the sun.

Photosynthesis was so successful that these tiny blue-green algae changed the earth's atmosphere with the 'waste' from its chemical reaction—oxygen. Over approximately four hundred million years these innumerable cyanobacteria flourished, increasing the amount of oxygen in the atmosphere from practically nothing to our current 21 percent. Though it was slow-moving, it was the

1

first climate crisis, as life had to adapt to its own corrosive waste, those higher concentrations of oxygen in the atmosphere.

Fast forward to the Devonian and Carboniferous eras between 350 and 150 million years ago, when giant forests and swamps covered the planet. What is now the province of Alberta, Canada was at that time a shallow, tropical sea, filled with photosynthetic algae and coral. In tandem with the forests that covered the land, they removed huge amounts of carbon dioxide from the atmosphere and the oxygen increased even more to an all-time high of 35 percent. This increase changed the climate again, and the earth cooled. The masses of dead trees and plants from those forests, swamps, and coral reefs were buried, sequestering that carbon taken from the atmosphere in deep geological layers of the earth. Over time, this organic biomass fossilized and transformed into natural gas, coal, and oil.

The Rise of Carbon Democracies

When wood burns, its fibres and minerals react with oxygen, and the carbon bound in its organic material gets released back into the atmosphere as carbon dioxide. The energy from the sun that went into growing the wood is released again, as heat, light, and ash.

Before the industrial revolution, most heat used for all sorts of processes was derived from wood or natural burnable material that needed sun power to grow. In his book *Carbon Democracy*, Timothy Mitchell argues that the timescale of energy and food production was dependent on the rate of photosynthesis in crops, the lifespan of animals, and the time needed to replenish stands of timber and grazing lands. This physical relationship with photosynthesis set certain limits to the socio-energetic metabolism of any society. A society seeking to increase its energy use could only do so by expanding available land use, and one way this was achieved was by colonizing more territory.

This all changed when humans obtained access to fossil fuels, first coal, then oil. Once we started burning fossil fuels at a large scale, humanity gained access to the energy from sunshine that had been buried over millions and millions of years. Since the industrial revolution in the mid-eighteenth century, we cracked open a cache of energy that had been accumulated over a massive amount of time and territory. That this could disturb "the harmony of the world" was already predicted by Eugène Huzar in 1857.

Coal was the primary fuel used in the steam-powered industry and petroleum was exclusively used for illumination. Electrification of streetlamps at the beginning of the 20th century made the use of oil redundant for lighting, so this was, according to Mitchell, a primary driver for switching to using oil for mechanical power, at first, to heat the water for steam-engine boilers and later in internal combustion engines, designed to run exclusively on oil. The internationalization of oil happened in even more recent history, after the termination of the second world war. The post-war US aid programs, which were designed to make Europe economically healthy as soon as possible, pushed Europe to change from coal to oil. Mitchell expertly analyses how this switch set our 20th-century democracies on track to becoming 'carbon democracies' together with a new macro-economic concept of calculating and managing the circulation of money tied to the movement of oil, now well-known as 'the economy.'

This new social-energetic metabolism decoupled the dependence of population centres on their immediate territory for energy provision. Thus, the stage was set for immense technological innovation in tandem with explosive population growth. This event is often called 'the great acceleration'. Could we view it this way: all this massively released energy has ultimately been converted into population mass? If so, the question becomes what happens when this population mass releases the sequestered carbon that was accumulated over 300 million years back into the atmosphere in just one big belch of only 300 years?

Climate Change

Change is a given in the evolution of our planet, and its biosphere operates within the envelope of the earth's system. To name our planet's living system, scientists refer to Greek mythology again: they call it Gaia, after the primordial goddess of Earth, mother of all life.

Gaia has gone through many eras of climatic change. Like the blue-green algae from archaic times, we are a hugely successful 'infestation' species, but we are ravishing the available resources on our planet and creating more waste than the ecosystem can handle.

What is happening now is unprecedented. There is a conundrum at the heart of the discussion surrounding climate change: in geological terms, this change is happening at warp speed. On a human scale, it is happening at a rate that is too slow to be alarming to many people. Climate change is a prime example of what Rob Nixon presents in his book, *Slow Violence and the Environmentalism of the Poor:* "By slow violence I mean a violence that occurs gradually and out of sight, a violence of destruction that is dispersed across time and space, an attritional violence that is typically not viewed as violence at all."

Climate change became a household term only recently, but scientists had been aware for some time that burning fuels could pose a problem, if not a threat. Early mentions of the issue include deforestation and air pollution from smoke in London, England, in writings from John Evelyn (1620-1706). In 1896, Svante Arrhenius was the first to calculate that fossil fuel combustion could eventually result in global warming. Concerns grew, and by 1988 the Intergovernmental Panel on Climate Change (IPCC) was established to prepare regular comprehensive reviews and recommendations concerning the state of knowledge of the science of climate change.

Here is what we know: Earth's average temperature will increase through the accumulation of trapped heat caused by an increased amount of carbon dioxide, methane, and nitrous oxide in the atmosphere, released through human action. That is why they have the collective name of greenhouse gases. The rise of average global temperature will have many effects: the permanent ice mass on the planet will continue to melt faster than it freezes, so sea levels will keep rising, flooding coastal population centres and small islands. The temperature change affects air and ocean circulation patterns, thereby causing tempestuous and massively destructive weather events: hurricanes, floods, droughts, and wildfires. The cascading effects will be disruptive to plant and animal life and to our ability to grow food. These changes will displace an even more massive number of people than they already have. The UN estimates 20 million people a year are displaced by climate change, resulting in a total of 1.2 billion by 2050. Uche Umezurike delves into environmental migration with his story "Fireflies" in this volume. These are only the main examples. There are many, many more subtle feedback effects that scientists are studying, and those insights are continuously updated, so our picture of this complex climate change system is constantly shifting. But one urgent conclusion remains unaffected: it is going to be a massive problem for humanity and if we don't immediately curb our output of greenhouse gases, we can reach a threshold at which the planet will no longer be able to sustain human life.

Time for Action

Here is what we also know: we must reduce our fossil fuel consumption. In our search for solutions, we immediately bump into multiple related issues which demonstrate we are dealing with a wickedly complex problem. One obvious solution points to making our technologies less carbon-intensive, by adapting existing technologies and inventing new ones. Finding alternative solutions has already been in motion for several decades and we are at a fortunate crossroads, where many renewable technologies have become viable options. Maggie Hanna has done an excellent job in outlining these solutions in, "How can the future go really, really well?" the last essay of this book.

The Russian invasion of Ukraine in 2022 is a shocking reminder that we haven't put the politics of empire and colony behind us and are causing another wave of human suffering as well as massive shortages of gas inflicted on Europe for its support of Ukraine. The world is collectively holding its breath, watching an accelerating development of renewables, and wondering what its outcome is going to be. It is a race to free us all from the very dependency on non-renewables that fed colonial thinking and led to climate change.

However, we need more than a technofix. We also must deal with pollution, depletion of natural resources and destruction of ecosystems. They are equally complex problems intertwined with climate change. Reducing our consumption is a necessity. We must move to a circular system where the 'waste' of one process becomes a resource for another. We can deconsume by buying less and using products that last a long time or are easy to repair. This is a sensible and productive course of action, with a much longer history than our current practices.

Further, as Natalie Meisner and Jacqueline Huskisson point out in their combination of incisive poetry and visual imagery titled "Clingwrap," we need to disabuse ourselves of the planetarily destructive absurdity of the idea that we need to package ourselves—and everything else—in plastic, or manufacture products with planned obsolescence to live a prosperous and hygienic life.

A flaw in our current economic model is to exempt its impact on nature as an 'externality'. This dematerializes the economy and creates the impression limitless growth is possible. The paradigm of limitless accumulation needs to be revoked because this thinking threatens to break the physical limits of our earth system. The loss of biodiversity on our planet over just the past 25 years is shocking. We are part of the web of life and by violating it, we violate ourselves. For example, insect populations are declining at such a rate it affects the pollination of our plants and food crops! Global action is shaping up after a Conference of the Parties to the UN Convention on Biological Diversity, called COP15, in Montreal in December 2022. The world has finally decided that a united effort for global conservation has the highest priority, and an agreement to protect at least 30 percent of our planet, has been reached. Many details are to be fleshed out, but a target to reduce the use of pesticides by half in 2030 has been set. One of the contributors to this book, Alice Major, was invited to come and read from her "Welcome to the Anthropocene" at the COP15 conference as part of programming at the Canada Pavilion. She was part of a panel discussion on the challenge of communicating science to non-scientists—a challenge that is also central to our project in this volume.

Oil is connected to extractivist thinking in which nature exists purely as a resource to be exploited. Indeed, being independent of nature is seen as the ultimate expression of freedom. We need to change that thinking to a more holistic worldview. Anthropologist Wade Davis is a great advocate to remind us that there are many different worldviews in existence, and that our dominant, industrial view in which non-human forces and systems have no place isn't the only possible one. For many Indigenous cultures, the land is alive, it is a sacred geography, and nature is animated. Different values and respect for the web of life nurture lifestyles that are more reciprocal and generative with the natural world. It is time to listen and learn from these non-exploitative, non-industrial cultures.

The planet's resources are being consumed at an unsustainable rate, but not evenly across the globe. We have a huge issue of equity in this debate. For example, the affluent cultures in Europe, North America, and Australia have the most carbon-intensive lifestyle and impact per capita. However, in Asia, human impact on climate change rests with numbers. A modest increase in the standard of living results in a carbon footprint amplified by the sheer size of its population. The acceleration in global consumption is highly unequal, and most humans continue to be denied their basic needs. People who struggle to survive, and there are many, don't have the luxury to worry about reducing their footprint. This inequality exists everywhere. Indigenous Peoples have been seeking social justice in demanding reconciliation with Canada's damaging settler, colonizing past. Involving Indigenous Peoples as equal partners and recognizing their right to free and prior informed consent in decisions regarding land rights and resource extraction are important components in tackling domestic climate justice.

But what we need is more than thought. In his poem, "A Foot Each in Two Canoes," Michael Leeb makes us feel the necessity of recognizing the connection between climate change and decolonizing our relationship with the Indigenous population of Canada. And in "Challenging Times," the bi-racial Kainai artist Jared Tailfeathers and ecologist Larry Kapustka connect six principles related to energy futures with six Blackfoot words or concepts and the traditional knowledge embedded into them. In this combination of sestina and essay, European and Indigenous views acknowledge a shared love for Gaia, Earth, and Turtle Island.

The Journey to Re-imagining Fire and Energy Futures

My childhood was steeped in oil and white privilege. Monica Kidd, Mark Hopkins, and others in this book also refer to growing up with the comfort of new inventions, while at the same time enjoying a world that was not yet as heavily degraded or polluted as ours has become. Ironically, the international lifestyle of my father's oil career exposed me to remote places, where I learned to love unspoiled parts of nature. These experiences have been foundational to me. Currently, I live and work in Calgary, Alberta, Canada. Looking back and reflecting on the necessity to change, I aim to create connections in my practice between art, science, biodiversity, social activism, and climate change.

This path has led to my Fellowship with the Energy Futures Lab (EFL) in 2018. The non-profit Lab is based in Alberta and consists of 40 to 60 Fellows and support staff. They are a network of innovators and influencers with diverse views and come from government and communities, the energy sector, First Nations, non-profits, academia, and the arts. The EFL supports change-makers as they collaboratively explore the following question: How can we leverage Canada's assets and innovation capacity to accelerate an inclusive and equitable transition to a prosperous net-zero future?

Alberta embodies a microcosm of issues that are encountered worldwide in the energy transition debate. Alberta, with most of its wealth derived from oil and gas, is steeped in today's still-dominant petro-culture. This relationship with fossil fuels creates resistance to change. However, being an oil and gas-producing region also means that there are many people already trained in working with energy technologies, making the transition into new jobs relatively easy. Alberta has a large Indigenous population with its own proud cultures, histories, and worldviews, struggling for general reconciliation with their colonized past and securing their place in a transitioning world. The province still has relatively wide tracts of wilderness. Alberta has a lot of potential for developing renewable energy, as it is rich in sun, wind, and geothermal heat. The province is rich in lithium brine which can be extracted from existing wells but has an issue with cleaning up old oil and gas infrastructure and toxic tailings from the oilsands. Though differently proportioned, these are challenges and opportunities encountered all over the globe, which makes the Alberta story a global story.

Combining my experience as a visual artist and a Fellow, I invited submissions from 40 Alberta printmakers, writers, and poets. I connected this diverse group, ranging from emerging to veteran artists and authors, through a series of networking sessions with Fellows from the EFL. Next, artists and writers were paired, and everyone participated in informational group sessions with the Fellows-experts, to learn about energy transition and be inspired. This project is completely Alberta-based. The resulting text and images are published as an original fine-art print portfolio in tandem with this book publication.

The book is intended to be visionary. Many people struggle with forming an idea of our future. Providing a vision through an artistic lens can inspire, empower, and feed action. The public is aware of the debate on climate change and the need for the energy transition. The uncertainty that follows from heading into new pathways with cultural changes has created a deeply divided debate on the direction of the transition. Many voices in this debate are from experts in industry, scientists, and policymakers. Visual images and literature can translate the technical talk of science into the emotional domain of public discourse. Artists cannot provide definitive answers or solutions, but they can envision, clarify, question, and experiment with the entangled narratives of the energy transition. This narrative involves change over a long timeline, which can also be bridged in storytelling. Stories and poems can rouse public sentiment in a way that scientific facts cannot.

The artists and writers were free to choose their subject matter, and it was enriching for me, as curator and editor, to reap fantastic results. Many go back to basics: the priority of protecting our natural environment and the necessity of having access to clean air, the soil of the earth, and water. Elements of nature. Mary Kavanagh has created a reflection of our complex atmosphere with lyrical simplicity: what is in the sky, and what is this materiality that we, and the whole world, are made of? Richard Harrison and Rosemary Griebel have written odes to the soil: Richard critiquing its sometimes-despised role in history, Rosemary, herself a gardener, explores our intimacy with it and the hope in regenerative farming. Carole Bondaroff depicts the constancy found in traditional and modern windmills, while Mar'ce Merrell invites a group of experts around a campfire to share their stories of water alongside the visual image of artist Liz Ingram's hands, which are holding water like prayer. In Tara Manyfingers' image of a colonized Narcissus gazing into a pool, we have a glimpse of how we should adore the clean water itself rather than our own reflection and our exploitative desires. In Emma Gammans' story, an impoverished couple illegally gathers firewood to keep warm. Kate Baillies and Katie Bruce pulled prints from physical matter: soil, grass, or a crack in the wall. Kasia Koralewska boiled natural fibres to make dye. The clouds and rocks in Jill Ho-You's cyanotype have a more menacing nature, as does the coal mining depicted by Alex Thompson.

The contributions to this book are incredibly honest. The authors openly share how they are wrestling with the complexities of our time and the fact that there are no easy answers. Alexis Kienlen and Kathryn Lennon muse on this when writing on energy poverty and growing your food. The supporting images by Heather Urness and Hannah Gelderman are playful linocuts and screenprints. Times of crisis are times of doubt for all, and readers will notice that supporters of the energy transition feel uncertainty too. The main character in Donna Williams' story wonders if her husband should switch to working in "the new nuclear"? And while many authors decry the damaging pollution resulting from oil extraction, they acknowledge they are also part of its culture. Jessica Semenoff depicts damaged fish in the Athabasca River. Poet Shannon Kernaghan feels 'slippery' between environmental criticism and her partner's work in oil and gas. Environmental care is often placed in opposition to a hypermasculine culture connected with the oil patch, indicating that a cultural shift needs to happen as an essential ingredient of energy transition. Peter Midgley tells an apocalyptic, surrealist story featuring an environmental pestilence with a connection to our recent pandemic. The story was triggered by the image of his paired artist, Stan Phelps.

Another strong theme in this book is hope. Alice Major, Kim Mannix, Maggie Hanna, and Barbara Howard all have hope for the future. In Alice Major's work, the earth we learned to break open is the lid of the Pandora's box of fossil fuels, but there is also hope left in the box and the earth, such as the green resource of geothermal heat. Sylvia Arthur has depicted it as a human pipeline, while Jamie-Lee Girodat shows the bowels of the earth as a mass of wriggling arms full of potential action. We need mindful action sustained by empathy, exercised on many levels. We need action from industry, regulation and stimulus from levels of government and awareness at a community and individual level, all with a willingness to support and make the changes that are possible in their sphere. Nadia Perna and I reflect on these many interlocking elements of transition; either like a patchwork blanket or facets constructed into a prism. Barbara tells a great epistolary story set in the future in which much has changed, but many things are still ordinarily the same. Her story is tinged with nostalgia, which is another theme that creeps into many contributions. In urging us to recognize we have a choice, Mark Hopkins explores two future scenarios: one which works out well, and one that doesn't. Even the dark story by Uche Peter Umezurike finds hope. He writes about a child-climate refugee, who invents a solution for the future. What is more hopeful than youth and imagination? There is always the possibility of an unexpected invention. Recent reports on fundamental breakthroughs in nuclear fusion are optimistic sparks for the future.

Hope, imagination, and action. Can they re-imagine fire not as the energy created by an Earth diminished by consumption, but as the feeding power of the wind and waves and the sun and the soil and the earth beneath? To re-imagine fire as Gaia's child and re-imagine our inventions as good for all living things, not just us. What we are transitioning to is not just a different way of doing old things, but moving from despair, dogmatism, and inactivity to hope, **imagination, and action.** To imagine is to dream in practical terms. And, as Chris Turner reminds us in his foreword and his recent book, *How to be a Climate Optimist*, the progress of new technologies is accelerating, to make our world not only sustainable but to make it even better. So, too, must our political and social will to use them.

—Bearspaw, December 2022

Recommended Reading

Davis, Wade. *The Wayfinders. Why Ancient Wisdom Matters in the Modern World.* Anansi Press, 2009

Gosh, Amitav. *The Great Derangement. Climate Change and the Unthinkable.* Chicago University Press, 2016

MacKinnon, J.B. *The Day the World Stops Shopping.* Random House Canada, 2021

Mitchell, Timothy. *Carbon Democracy. Political Power in the Age of Oil.* Verso, 2011

Nixon, Rob. *Slow Violence and the Environmentalism of the Poor.* Harvard University Press, 2011

Turner, Chris. *How to be a Climate Optimist. Blueprints for a Better World.* Random House Canada, 2022

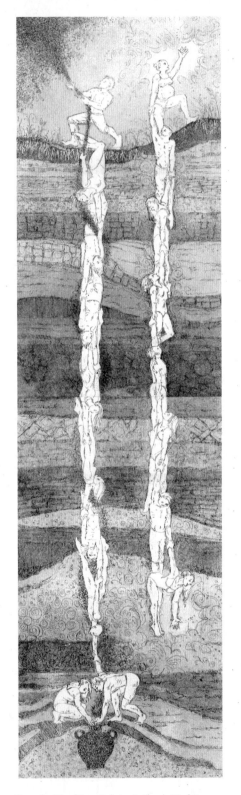

People Pipeline, Sylvia Arthur. Etching.
Artist's statement is at the end of this chapter.

CHAPTER ONE

SOMETIMES YOU HAVE TO DIG...

Alice Major, Author
Sylvia Arthur, Artist

Hi, Sylvia!

I'm trying to think through our project. We've been charged with expressing hope—to look at the ways people are tackling climate change and making our shared art out of it. But I remember our first tentative conversation after you and I had started the research. "Do you feel hopeful?" you asked. And I had to say, "No, not really." Climate change seems so huge, so amorphous. It's like punching a fog that would never notice our individual efforts. Honestly, I have moments of wanting to subside into my own tiny life, hoping the fog will just somehow blow away.

But then, after we started learning about carbon capture and geothermal energy, you said something like, "Maybe we should be looking underground." Suddenly an image from old myth came to me—Pandora's box. It wasn't actually a box, originally. It was a pithos, a giant clay jar used for storing oil or wine. This particular pithos, given by the gods, had been stored with all the ills afflicting humanity, and when Pandora opened it, they all flew out—grief and sickness, anger and pain. But at the very bottom, there was hope, and it's still there.

Sometimes, when you need hope, you have to dig for it.

• • •

I like to think of all the layers beneath our feet—all the soils and sands and rocks that Earth has wrapped around her warm heart. Here in Alberta, we're standing on some of the oldest rocks on the planet—the North American craton—covered by layers of debris from mountain-building and sediments from a vast inland sea that sloshed in and out as the craton drifted slowly northward and land rose or sank again. Over millions of years, marine life, plants and ancient animals lived plentifully and died in the warm waters. Their carbon bodies were compressed under dust from new mountains that fractured the western horizon and then eroded again

Now we stand on this vast Western Canada Sedimentary Basin. Below us, layers interlock like fingers in a child's hand-stacking game: the Belly River formation ... Upper Mannville shale ... Wabamun muds ... the Leduc reef formation. A bewildering geological maze where those ancient life forms have metamorphosed into the coal, oil and gas we dig up to power our lives.

And where we begin to realize that what we have dug up is not the unqualified good we thought it was—that the carbon we have let out of the box and burned is heating up our planet's surface.

• • •

Pandora's jar was meant to be a punishment. The gods had been angered by the theft of their fire by Prometheus, craftsman and creator of humans—including that first woman, Pandora herself. The story goes that she was dressed up in nice clothes and sent down to create havoc, along with that closed jar.

Sure, blame the woman. Pandora got her bad rap from the poet Hesiod, writing in the eighth century BCE. However, there are other versions of the story in which she isn't named as the idiot who opened that jar and let all hell loose on humankind. And some scholars suggest that she was originally a very different figure—an ancient mother-earth goddess—and that her name means the giver (not the receiver) of all gifts. On a fifth-century amphora the half-figure of Pandora emerges from the ground, her arms upraised, as though she is the Earth.

It seems a bit strange to be dragging a myth from ancient Greece to a landscape where it doesn't belong. Pandora comes from the Western narratives that pervaded this realm and overlaid the spiritual understandings of the people who were here first. Indigenous Peoples can point to many other stories that grew here. They understand the world as a series of reciprocal, cyclical relationships with all life forms ("all my relations") rather than invention and control.

But I can't appropriate their stories. This is the one I was given. So, having brought this story here, maybe we should try to understand it. Pandora's myth is, at heart, a lesson in humility. We are very small, but small unintended actions can have huge consequences. We let things out that we can't easily put back.

• • •

Still, we can try. That's why it's inspiring to learn about carbon sequestration and the very real pipeline system that is tucking liquified carbon dioxide back into the rocks it came from—the formation that kept gas safely sealed away for millions of years. The Alberta Carbon Trunkline Project is collecting the CO_2 from various industrial processes—making fertilizer, processing bitumen, even brewing beer—and compressing it into a thick liquid. This is pumped through the pipeline to an old oilfield and then down 1800 metres into the geosphere. Through layers of Colorado shale ... through the Upper Nisku formation with its anhydrous salts ... through the shales and clays of the Ireton formation ... finally to fill the holes and channels in the Nisku limestone that sits below all this and is sealed off by the layers above it.

I do find this inspiring. Looking at the geology and the monitoring, I feel confident this will work. It will keep carbon dioxide from reaching the atmosphere, 1.5 million tonnes of it every year when the pipeline is at full capacity. This is real.

But it's still only a teaspoon in a large lake. Unless we drastically reduce the amount of fossil fuel we're burning to energize our homes, vehicles, industries, we're not going to moderate climate change. However, even a world plated with solar panels and twirling with windmills won't be enough to deliver the energy needed by 10 billion people in 2050.

This summer has already been so dominated by the whiplash of drought and flood from Cornwall to China. Warming air soaking up ever more moisture, then squeezing it out in great torrents. Time is shortening. We need to look deeper.

• • •

Then I think again of where we're standing. Not just here in Alberta, but on the surface of a planet with energy at its heart. Not simply the sips and pools of long-gone life, but the enormous heat at Earth's centre.

This is the oldest warmth of all, primordial, from the time when material in the planetary disk around the newly formed sun was pulled together by gravity. Everything from atoms to asteroids was banging around, and the swirling kinetic energy was transformed to heat. Add to that the deep, ongoing, radioactive decay of elements like uranium. Far below our feet, a thick shell of molten rock forms the mantle that surrounds the planet's core. Worldwide, this geothermal energy percolates slowly to the surface—even below the Antarctic's ice caps, and certainly here below Alberta.

So I am inspired by another project that is tapping into that geothermal energy. There's a modest demonstration project near Rocky Mountain House that's creating a kind of radiator to bring heat to the surface. Most geothermal projects have been based on capturing the heat from underground water or brine, which requires very specific kinds of geology to work. But the demonstration project consists of a pair of 2.5-km-deep boreholes connected at the bottom by a tunnel. A fluid circulates through this U-shaped path, harvesting heat from the rock itself and carrying it to a heat exchanger at the surface. The circulation doesn't need to be powered by pumps; it simply depends on the central fact that heat rises. The plant has been in operation since 2019, showing that the system does work and could be scaled up to commercial size, to heat buildings and power turbines. And it produces no CO_2!

I often feel like we're in one of those adventure movies where a car is racing against a train to reach a crossing in time. Could we implement a technology like this fast enough to make the difference we need in global levels of carbon dioxide? Then I think of how quickly technology can change things. The first automotive vehicles were cobbled together by inventors in the late 1890s. Within two decades they were common. Now we have to race against the automobile itself (and the planes and coal-fired generating stations) to make the fundamental changes we need in a very short time.

• • •

Back to Pandora's jar. The shape of the pithos reminds me of a womb, the primordial origin for all humans. The giant pottery jars were also used for death, to bury bones and bodies in Bronze Age Greece. Birth and death—that rhythm reminds me a little of warmth rising and falling in the geothermal loop. To me, it offers hope for a cycle that can be sustained.

• • •

Alice Major's 12th book of poetry, Knife on Snow, *reflects on the ecology and history of western Canada and beyond. She is also the author of the essay collection,* Intersecting Sets: A Poet Looks at Science. *Alice served as first poet laureate of Edmonton and founder of the Edmonton Poetry Festival.*

SOMETIMES YOU HAVE TO DIG FOR HOPE

Alice Major

Here on the planet's crust, so close
to the desperate cold of space,
we looked for warmth and rummaged
in the chest of wonders
we'd been gifted. We learned to burn—
crackle and spark of wood, its cooling ash.

We let things out from underground.
        They looked like hope
at first—coal's black gleam. The shine
of oil, its flair and freedoms. Only to find
we'd let loose ills and demons
in faint wisps of carbon gas that joined the air,
tipped it towards disaster.

Now we huddle together, try to tuck
some of that CO2 away, back
into the planet's rocky chest,
like children trying to conceal the mess
they've made. It's hard to hope
that this will be enough.

Still, deep in the giant jar of Earth
is all the warmth we'd need, welling
upward from the planet's core,
its molten mantle. We could dig down
again, with careful fingers,
to let that heat creep up from rock
to spin our turbines and exchange
our feckless combustions
for steady energy, stored hope.

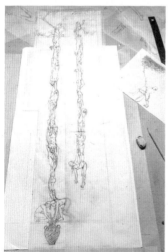 

People Pipeline art in process. Top: *People Pipeline* (detail), etching.
Bottom, left to right, Image design and inking the copper plate.
Sylvia Arthur.

PEOPLE PIPELINE
Etching on Kozuke paper, 2022, 33 x 96.5 cm.

Sylvia Arthur

STATEMENT

It might be challenging to consider climate change without feeling overwhelmed and powerless, yet improvements in energy transition that provide hope for a brighter future are on the horizon. The visual component of this artistic collaboration tells a story that is inspired by recent technological developments in Geothermal Energy and Carbon Capture Sequestration (CCS). The etching is an imaginary cross-section of the earth's underground rock layers, showing how depleted oil and gas infrastructure and geological formations are being used to support new energy advancements. Linked human figures depict a pipeline of CO2 being sequestered deep into the earth, while another chain of figures symbolically gathers Geothermal Energy from the earth's sub-terrestrial strata, bringing it up to the surface. The "People Pipeline" is a metaphor of humanity working together, hand in hand, to make positive changes for the future.

• • •

Sylvia Arthur is a graduate of the Visual Communications program at Alberta College of Art + Design (now Alberta University of the Arts) with extended studies in painting, drawing, and printmaking. Her work has a narrative aspect inspired by stories or poetry. She has designed exhibits (for example, Dinosaur Provincial Park) as well as public art in various Alberta locations. Other collaborative projects include the "Print(ed) Word," displayed at The Calgary Central Library.

Community, Jared Tailfeathers.
Acrylic on canvas reproduced as digital print on archival paper.
Artist's statement is at the end of this chapter.

CHAPTER TWO

CHALLENGING TIMES

Larry Kapustka, Author
Jared Tailfeathers, Artist

AN ENERGY FUTURES
SESTINA

Climate change and human population expansion
requires smart Innovation (iksimm)
if we are to achieve Resiliency (sskona'ta'pssi).
While there is much focus on energy technologies,
all would be wise to nurture culture's Power (Saaa'm)
as we search for sustainable Opportunities (waatoyinnayi),
because efficient energy, devoid of arts
makes a sterile Community (aaka'itapissko)
not worthy of the Change (isawa').
Physical and cultural landscapes have always
been subject to Change (isawa').
Humans have a gift enabling them to Innovate (iksimm),
to choose to be in harmony with the ways of nature,
to form vibrant Community (aaka̠'itapissko),
to be adaptable and respectful in striving
toward Resiliency (sskona'ta'pssi).
This is the challenge of our day,

to seize the Opportunity (waatoyinnayi)

to diversify varied forms of energy and

embrace emotional and cultural Powers (Saaa'm).

Fescue grasslands, for millennia, furnished Blackfoot

their source of solar Power (Saaa'm).

Decadal weather patterns modulated productivity

requiring vigilance of Change (isawa').

Observed phenology forecasts Opportunity (waatoyinnayi).

When old ways were not working,

it was necessary to Innovate (iksimm).

The wise, the observant, those with measured daring

became Resilient (sskona'ta'pssi).

From this, and by emulating wolf,

the Blackfoot developed Community (aaka'itapissko).

Nature has revealed models that are useful

for human forms of Community (aaka'itapissko)

that respect dynamics, that wisely nurture Power (Saaa'm),

that can foster cultural identity built for Resiliency (sskona'ta'pssi).

We can all learn from Indigenous Peoples

about how to adapt to Change (isawa'),

to incorporate new ways of thinking,

of using, of being, derived through Innovation (iksimm).

providing all peoples with great Opportunity,

Adapting to new economies creates Opportunity (waatoyinnayi).

Managing energy in forms of food is embedded

in Community (aaka'itapissko).

Success depends on Innovation (iksimm).

Sun, wind, and water again are the sources of Power (Saaa'm).

The ways of the buffalo (iinnii Bison bison)

and wolf can show the ways for Change (isawa'),

achieving for all peoples, Resiliency (sskona'ta'pssi).

Generational respect can teach us to be Resilient (sskona'ta'pssi)
and bring with it immense Opportunity (waatoyinnayi).
Embracing reconciliation demands transitional Change (isawa'),
reinstalling pride within Communities (aaka'itapissko)
and fostering unity of purpose for increasing Power (Saaa'm),
such that cultural integrity is strengthened
through Innovation (iksimm).
While seeking a new world order designed
to be Resilient (sskona'ta'pssi),
we will be required to engage and respect
our diverse Communities (aaka'itapissko).
This will necessitate uncommon courage
to embrace Opportunity (waatoyinnayi)
in ways that have seldom been done to harness
our enormous collective Power (Saaa'm).
There will be resistance and fear of Change (isawa')
as well as excitement that comes from
imagining new ways to achieve Innovations (iksimm).

• • •

We chose a specific poetic form known as a sestina as the vehicle for our message. A sestina consists of six lines per stanza and six stanzas. The lines are arranged in a specific pattern so that the last word rotates and will occupy all six positions. This poetic format originated in France in the 12th Century. Recently, Joy Harjo, Poet Laureate in the USA likened the structure to that of Navajo weavings. After producing the sestina, we elaborated each term to embrace the imperatives of reconciliation and explored the complex social-ecological systems inherent in energy transition.

Work on this piece began with the identification of six words we deemed central to the consideration of energy futures. In selecting the six words, we sought to reflect on traditional knowledge of Indigenous Peoples of what is now southern Alberta that could guide the transition that is before us. The words we chose (and the Blackfoot equivalent) were Power (Saaa'm), Change (isawa'), Opportunity (waatoyinnayi), Innovate (iksimm), Resilient (sskona'ta'pssi), and Community (aaka'itapissko).

1. Power (Saaa'm)

Power comes in many forms in our biophysical world. Unharnessed power comes in the form of storms, floods, fires, earthquakes, and volcanoes. These phenomena engender awe, perhaps differently in the past than today as we have learned something about these forces of nature through science.

Prior to the industrial revolution of the 18th and 19th centuries, power used by humans was limited mostly to brawn and domesticated animals harnessed to do work. That changed with the development of machines. Arguably the most substantive change resulting from machines was the attitude within non-indigenous societies that humans could live apart from the forces of nature, that humans wielded control over all things. Such arrogance has led to destructive practices that present danger to human societies across the globe and threaten multiple assemblages of plants and animals with extinction.

The industrial revolution spawned many developments, not the least being scientific discoveries in public health. Implementing policies and practices has resulted in longer life expectancy due to fewer infant and early childhood deaths. While death rates declined, birth rates remained the same resulting in a burgeoning human population globally. The expanding population spread geographically, usually to the detriment of Indigenous Peoples.

The effects of colonization are profound. In the prairies of North America, Indigenous Peoples lived in a solar-powered system. The bison have been described as the "batteries" that stored the sun's energy in the form of food and fibre transported across the prairies and harvested for human use. For several millennia the ebb and flow of plant and animal productivity governed the fortunes of the tribal communities. Coincident with colonization, the wanton slaughter of bison upended the lifestyle of these Indigenous Peoples. Disease and perverse attitudes, including the Doctrine of Discovery, resulted in genocidal actions that decimated populations of Indigenous Peoples. With that, much of the experiential knowledge of living within the means of the natural systems was lost. Only now are we collectively learning the price of losing that knowledge.

Ecosystems provide food and fibre for humans. There is richness in the diversity of plants and animals that adapt and evolve in response to each other and the prevailing climate. Indigenous Peoples respect the diversity and recognize the healing power of different plants. Some plants are used in ceremony, some are observed as harbingers of seasons. All these forms of power, or medicines (Saaa'm), informed the way of life on the prairies.

As we lurch toward the middle of the 21st century, power occurs both as control exercised over others or a type of energy. The primary sources of energy that drove the industrial revolution were fossil fuels (coal, petroleum, natural gas), which have brought on the forces of climate change resulting in destabilizing weather and ecological systems. The realization that human societies are in jeopardy is triggering development of new sources of energy (solar, wind, geothermal, nuclear). But these are being approached in many cases as singular, engineering solutions. We would be wise to focus on the interconnectedness of our complex social-ecological systems and adopt holistic approaches that consider power in the broadest sense.

2. Change (isawa')

Social-ecological systems change over time. Nothing is constant. Economic structures, whether based on barter or agreed value of some currency are challenged if change occurs rapidly or sporadically. During the days when hunter-gatherer societies were prominent, bands experienced periods of abundance and episodes of crippling shortages caused by droughts, floods, or other calamities.

Historical events with global consequences include volcanic eruptions such as Mounts Mazama, Vesuvius, and Krakatoa. Injection of ash into the upper atmosphere reduced the intensity of solar radiation reaching Earth's surface resulting in several years of cooler temperatures. We know from archaeological evidence exposed at Head-Smashed-in Buffalo Jump, a UNESCO site in southern Alberta, that there was a gap of a millennium or more in usage of the site as a buffalo jump, possibly due to a shift in migration routes of the bison.

Modern societies also are subject to social-ecological disruptions. In addition to the ebbs and flows of climate, contemporary economies face additional stresses that disrupt the flow of goods and services, along the global supply chain. Our contemporary "poster child" for such disruption is the Covid-19 pandemic that exposed deficiencies in food, water, and energy distribution systems. The Russian invasion of Ukraine has blocked transport of grains to Africa and other regions and threatens widespread famine.

And, we are currently experiencing disruptions from human-induced climate change. Crop failures due to heat, drought, fires, floods, and outbreaks of diseases jeopardize food security in many regions. The pace of change poses challenges that are playing out on global scales unlike any that humans have experienced previously.

Consensus is that combustion of fossil fuels (coal, petroleum, natural gas) is responsible for the rise in atmospheric carbon dioxide. This, plus releases of methane, constitute the two most potent greenhouse gases that lead to atmospheric warming and acidification and warming of oceans. These factors are linked to disrupted weather patterns including increased frequency and intensity of severe events. The abruptness of the shifting weather patterns places stress on food production at all levels from home gardening to intensive agriculture.

Consequently, human societies can expect unprecedented

change in how we generate and use energy. Competing economic and political factions are already engaged in vigorous policy debates regarding the urgency of the moment and the appropriate pace of transition—the intensity of the debate will likely increase.

3. Opportunity (waatoyinnayi)

Crises, though difficult to experience, can signal opportunities. When the bison changed migration patterns, presumably in response to shifts in weather that affected habitat quality, Indigenous Peoples altered their hunting strategies. Throughout history, challenges have been visited on all societies. The current climate crisis provides opportunities for our time. It is a time for reflection, re-examination, exploration, and action.

During the past 400 years, industrial societies became reliant on fossil fuels; for the last 100 years petroleum has supplied most of our energy. Penetration of railroads across North America, powered in large part by coal, was linked to the demise of the massive bison herds that roamed the plains.

Reliance on fossil fuels has resulted in highly mechanized, industrialized agriculture that uses petroleum to fuel and lubricate behemoth machines, provide fertilizers and pesticides, pump surface and fossil water to crops, and long-distance transport of crops to markets. It has also promoted private transportation in lieu of public transit, especially in North America. The backbone of the petroleum industry is composed of heavily subsidized multinational corporations and disproportionate leverage over government policies.

Warnings about the causal relationship between fossil fuels and climate change started two centuries ago. Physicists and climatologists became more vocal about these threats more than 40 years ago. Today, there is widespread agreement that human-induced climate change is due largely to the consumption of fossil fuels. Other human behaviours such as deforestation and other land use practices contribute to the crisis as well.

Globally, societies are seeing the threat of climate change as a catalyst to change, as an invitation to explore new opportunities in how we harness and use energy. Opportunities exist across the spectrum of policy, technology, and behaviour. Whether we succeed or not will be measured in how we evaluate opportunities that embrace comprehensive innovation and what actions we take.

4. Innovate (iksimm)

There are three components that determine the success of innovation. Namely, policy, technology, and behaviour.

Policy: Communities and nations can set policies that can have profound effects on energy choices and usage. At the highest levels of government, innovation can be built into tax structures as well as subsidies and stimulus packages to industrial sectors. Municipalities can enact bylaws affecting building codes, or restrictions on energy types. Requirements for building public facilities to Platinum LEED standards are being implemented. Zoning restrictions, including limiting urban sprawl to protect quality agricultural lands, can be highly effective.

Corporations have a substantive role to play in setting internal policies aimed at lowering energy consumption. Setting near-term and long-term targets for reducing carbon footprints is becoming commonplace. Industry and professional associations can play a significant role toward innovation.

One of the most significant challenges to policy change that encourages innovation is centred on equitable access. Historically, the benefits from advances in technology tend to go to the most affluent, further widening the gap between the haves and the barely-haves. Remote rural communities, including most Indigenous populations, must be afforded access to and reap the benefits of innovations and be innovators themselves. That is a responsibility of government and of corporations as they strive to obtain and retain their social licence to operate.

Technology: The past decade has seen great advances in energy technology. Some of the advance comes from improvements in older technologies made feasible through economies of scale. This is perhaps most pronounced in three forms of renewable energy: solar, wind, and geothermal. In each of these sectors, prices have continued to come down to levels that are below the costs of energy production for petroleum and natural gas.

Opportunities for innovation exist in the placement of infrastructure and in decentralizing the generation and distribution of electricity. Microgenerators, primarily solar panel installation on homes and businesses, can play a major role in diversifying energy production. And they have value in urban and rural settings.

Battery technology is advancing rapidly, including rapid recharging stations. Areas ripe for innovation include extending the life of batteries, minimizing end-of-life wastes, and reducing the footprint related to accessing lithium. A promising development in Alberta is the extraction of lithium from abandoned oil wells.

Behaviour: The third prong of innovation may be the most important in our quest to combat climate change. Jevons Paradox, named after the British economist William Stanley Jevons, advanced in 1865, states that as steam boilers became more efficient, the total consumption of coal would increase. An update of this concept by Joseph Tainter in 2008 concluded that Jevons Paradox is applicable across the board. For example, increased fuel efficiency in automobiles led to greater total consumption of gasoline. Relieved of the guilt of driving a gas guzzler, people are prone to take more and longer trips. Or those who previously could not afford to own a personal car determined they could with the greater fuel economy. Economists refer to this as a "rebound effect."

If individually or collectively we fail to lower wasteful use, and instead generate more electricity, get more electrical gadgets, and drive our electric vehicles greater distances, we risk the reversal of all the gains we worked so hard to attain.

5. Resilient (sskona'ta'pssi)

All extant life is testament to an innate drive for survival. Through some combination of fitness and chance, every living creature is the product of resiliency. Yet, due to the profound, oversized influence humans have exerted, Mother Earth is experiencing the 6th wave of mass extinctions. The forces, the power, the dominance of humans is stretching the coping capacity of plants and animals. We do not know what the break point is for human societies. We have a sacred obligation to act in ways that safeguard not only human society, but importantly our fellow travelers. Might we be more likely to nurture resiliency if we adopted the perspective of Indigenous Peoples as they refer to the "plant people" and the "animal people?"

We understand from western science that resiliency is an attribute of complex ecological systems. Unfortunately, we do not yet know which parts of these systems are needed to keep them functioning. So, as we combat climate change by shifting toward renewable energy, we need to be aware of relationships within the social-ecological systems and be humble about what we do not know and may never know. Amidst all the disruptive forces operating today geopolitically and economically, society is engaging in several grand experiments to transition away from dependence on fossil fuels. We seem to be operating under the tacit assumption that if we shift entirely to renewable forms of energy that we will save society.

But that is a dangerous assumption. Unless a holistic transformation occurs, we are not likely to maintain resiliency. We need much more than an engineering solution. We need to nurture a shift in perspectives that recognizes the interconnectedness within complex social-ecological systems. That requires changes in attitudes toward nature, changes in behaviours, openness to diversity in all forms. Only then will we be poised to maintain resilient societies.

6. Community (aaka'itapissko)

Social-ecological systems are composed of communities of individuals having common interests, common aspirations, and common heritage. We know from ecological studies that the structure of any community is the result of its past and it is dynamic; there is a memory of the past that determines the trajectory of the community as it develops. Although Indigenous Peoples model their culture in part on the circle, that should not be interpreted as returning to the past, but rather having awareness of the past. Current conditions are different and can never be recreated to be exactly as they once were. Yet, the idea of cycles, whether seasonal or generational, has utility in understanding who we are and where we might be headed. We ought not expect a return to the time when bison roamed freely across the plains in great numbers. But that should not deter us from re-establishing enclaves with viable bison herds and re-introducing wolves and beaver and other culturally important species if for no other reason than to be touchstones to the past. To not do so would be to deny future generations the opportunity to experience at least some segment of their heritage.

The quest for renewable energy requires more than technological breakthroughs. There needs to be strong connections to social systems as well. And increasingly we understand what many Indigenous Peoples knew for millennia: the welfare of humans is bound inextricably to our ecological surroundings. Humans are not above nor below other components of the ecological system. They are equals.

That perspective of being embedded in and not apart from nature informed the development of Indigenous human community and is understood to have been critical to survival. Wolf, for instance, played a foundational role in the organization and function of the Blackfoot community. After observing wolf packs, how they behaved, how they hunted, the Blackfoot learned how to survive in the harsh conditions of the high plains of what is now western Alberta.

WOLF: MY SISTER, MY BROTHER
SESTINA

Larry Kapustka
in collaboration with Jared Tailfeathers

A mighty creature roams wild expanses with its pack,
all powerful.
Bellies full of mother's milk and meat scraps,
pups bound playfully.
Light of a full moon dancing through forest branches
evokes a howling lament.
Surely, this eerie penetrating cacophony fuels fears of
this awesome beast that is so misunderstood.
First light on a frigid October morn,
illuminates silvery hackles of a male, so enchanting.
Its place among companion animals and plants,
prey and sustenance, is that of a keystone species.

Natural assemblages are what they are due
to the influence of keystone species.
Although individually strong, as a pack the wolf
is especially powerful.
Standing on the crest of a prairie hillock the
alpha male truly is enchanting.
Self awareness of strength and hierarchical position
allows the pack to be playful.
As the wolf's behavior is largely peaceful,
its place among us is grossly misunderstood.
Sensing this, is the
night-song of wolf a lament?

Or is it humans who should express lament?
For so dishonouring the role of this keystone species.
For fashioning outlandish myths
that demonstrate how maddingly
wolf is misunderstood?
This despite lessons we could learn
from brother wolf that are so powerful.
Lessons that we could learn how to relax
when our needs have been met and be playful.
Were we to adopt the teachings from sister wolf,
might we become equally special/enchanting?

The goal should not be to claim dominance,
but to earn respect for being special;
To live our lives with honour and respect so that
we have little to lament;
To create space for leisure, to enjoy all that is around us,
and to be playful;
To adopt the manner of a keystone species;
To achieve a balance of kindness and
sharing commensurate with being powerful.
In these ways, we can reduce
the chances of being misunderstood.

Efforts to learn from plant and animal people
are often misunderstood.
But of the straight trunk of lodgepole pine,
what could be more enchanting.
The ways of learning from wolf people are powerful.

When these cohabitants of ours are diminished,
there is much to lament.
The regulatory strength of brother wolf underscores
its role as a keystone species.
Yet we see that even with their power and elegance,
they teach us to be playful.

Hubris denies us of our ability to be playful.
Our role in the complex ecological system
is so often misunderstood.
Destruction of landscapes is more aligned
with virulent parasites than of keystone species.
Pomposity is honoured above the humility of
simply being special.
For this we truly have much to lament.
Human drive for dominion over the lands is destructive,
a false sense of being powerful.

• • •

In the spirit of reconciliation, we owe each other the respect of learning about the diverse cultures, the varied communities across this landscape. Perhaps the most important lesson we can learn, and embrace is that to have a livable environment, we need to live within our means. We need to understand that economies are one aspect of viable society; that societies, composed of communities, are embedded within and wholly dependent on the flow of goods and services from ecological systems.

The viability of the communities at minimum is determined by the quality of the ecological system measured in terms of access to food, fibre, and clean water. But humans require more. There must be access to sacred sites as governed by cultural norms and to recreational opportunities. While we

reimagine ways to generate energy, we owe our future generations a platform that enhances their quality of life in the form
that enables continued innovation to build resilient, diverse,
respectful communities.

• • •

*Larry Kapustka is an emeritus senior ecologist. He marvels at the
intricacies of social-ecological systems and understands that we must be
humble about what we think we know. His work has allowed extensive
travel across North America, Europe, as well as portions of Africa and
Asia Pacific. In retirement, he lives on an acreage with his wife Susan
Kristoferson, an artist, where he raises chickens, and enjoys hunting and
fishing. Larry was a founding member of the Foothills Energy Coop as
well as the Diamond Valley Sustainable Living Centre for which he serves
as chair.*

Counterclockwise from top:
Power, Change, Innovate, Resilient, Opportunity, Jared Tailfeathers.
Pencil and marker and acrylic on canvas.

COMMUNITY (aaka'itapissko) *AND INNOVATE* (iksimm)
Acrylic paint on canvas, 2022, 27.9 x 35.56 cm.

POWER (Saaa'm), *CHANGE* (isawa'), *OPPORTUNITY*
(waatoyinnayi), *RESILIENT* (sskona'ta'pssi)
Pencil and marker on paper, 2022, 21.6 cm x 27.9 cm.

Jared Tailfeathers

STATEMENT

Indigenous Peoples have been close to nature since time imme-
morial. Physical landmarks, as well as the plants and animals
that live on these lands, are woven throughout the culture of
Indigenous Peoples. Misuse and even destruction of these parts
of our land in effect are destructive to ourselves and our way of
life. Learning from the ways animals interact became the foundation of Indigenous Culture, one that resulted in a small carbon
footprint. In particular, wolf informed the Blackfoot on ways to
hunt as a group and is reflected in our origin stories. Similarly,
the Buffalo or Bison is the most important animal in all the Plains
cultures; losing them is how we lost ourselves, our language, culture, and land. The disappearance of these two keystone animals
changed history and the land. The Blackfoot and other Indigenous
Peoples view the return of these animals and their connection to
Indigenous cultures to have major importance toward living in
harmony and within the means provided by these lands.

• • •

Jared Tailfeathers is a multidisciplinary, bi-racial Blackfoot (Kainai) artist,
musician, inventor, workshop facilitator/teacher, amateur Historian/
researcher, and author. He builds original musical instruments for
interactive projects, performances, workshops, recording, and for sale. He
works in various styles, media, genres, and materials depending on the
project or commission.

Cycle, Kasia Koralewska. Silkscreen.
Artist's statement is at the end of this chapter.

CHAPTER THREE

ON THE LURE OF MULTIPLE INSTANCES

Monica Kidd, Author
Kasia Koralewska, Artist

I GREW UP A CHILD OF THE SEVENTIES on the Alberta prairies. We were a couple of hundred people in a bustling Canadian National Railway whistle-stop. The summers were long, the distances vast. If you weren't a farmer, you were someone whose small business relied on them.

I can remember a time without pumpjacks, their arrival in a field signalling some mysterious new kind of wealth like a limo rolling down main street. Someone with deep pockets wielding information that stood to change the way we saw our own land. My dad spoke proudly of mineral rights and royalty cheques, and this puzzled me. My Alberta was sagebrush and dust and snakes and birds and the swoosh of bruised knees through long grass. Why we needed to learn anything below the organic soil layer was beyond me.

Perhaps as we age, we become better able to contemplate invisible things. But when I was still young, my father took me to the nearby excavation of an Edmontonsaurus specimen. It was a moment of fame for our area, and it marked a time when I began to understand that the ground beneath our feet was something that didn't belong to us. It belonged to history, or it belonged to the creatures—the people—who had come before. We were evolution's buzzing flies. We mattered. Of course we mattered. How we experienced the fragile, dew-kissed world mattered. How we treated each other and our places mattered very much.

Of course, I didn't understand the economics involved, how people needed pay cheques to keep the farm afloat, how oil—all those impossibly old little compressed organic bodies—from Alberta's murky depths powered ships to China and built our hospital and brought me my Saturday morning cartoons. I still don't, not really. But I accepted that these things were true.

I went off to university to become an ecologist. I read Rachel Carson and Edward Abbey—realistic romantics who watched the world with the discipline of scientists but loved it unapologetically with big sloppy kisses. I learned about Manifest Destiny, the idea employed to justify crimes committed in the settling of the West and wondered how this influenced my own lineage of settlers. I joined the student environmental movement. I organized demonstrations and conferences. I cut off my hair and stopped eating meat. I threatened never to come home again if my dad turned unbroken land he owned into a golf course. (He did; I relented.)

Decades passed. That Alberta's oil powers ships and builds hospitals and funds creative work is more fathomable to me. But knowing what I know now about the side effects of fossil fuels, it is just as unsettling. I don't believe we can simply walk away from oil. We cannot one day just wake up and privilege one form of technology over another, dust off our hands and go for beers, dragging with us the same old attitudes and political structures, and what Irish philosopher Iris Murdoch calls the "unambiguous optimism ... [that is] part of the Anglo-Saxon tradition." Maturing toward sustainability will require enduring a likely long and awkward adolescence.

One thing we will need to face, I believe, is the lure of multiple instances. I muck about with letterpress printmaking, and something that can set printmaker social media channels abuzz is trying to figure out exactly what is so compelling about a stack of prints, a stack of books, any stack of nearly identical things. The evolutionary biologist in me wants to say it's about ferreting out the small differences that might mean the success of one thing over the other, that show the hand of the maker. Or perhaps that multiple-made objects adopt the strategy of broadcast spawning: each instance carries an infinitely small opportunity to touch a life, but a small number multiplied is at least a chance. Multiple instances are the product of the industrial will. Not all things require oil, but access to cheap energy drives our ability to keep making—and consuming—more.

But these are just games of metaphor. We also love multiples because we worship abundance, and not just in a hedonistic way. We are biological creatures living in community with other biological creatures. The murmuration of starlings, or a school of fish flinching as one, or the Brownian motion of human crowds moving through Times Square, inspires awe because in those moments we know we are small, but we are not alone.

What I am trying to say is that abundance carries moral complexity. An industrial world fueled by oil has given us uniformity, predictability, and universality. To pretend it has not also given us instability and conflict is to carry on in the tradition of manifest destiny. I want a different future. I want a different present. I want to believe we can stop fighting over whose oil is greener, and how many atmospheric degrees, or inches of coastline, or thousands of salmon we can claw back by buying this car or supporting that pipeline. As we collectively feel our way through the energy transition, we will need to reconcile what kinds of abundance we can keep and which we will need to move past.

"Fix," my poem included in this collection, inhabits the moment of the awkward adolescence of the energy transition. It begins with nostalgic attention to a pumpjack on a spent well and a kind of grief for my father and his love of open roads. The pumpjack is a concrete image of late 20th-century prairies, but here also symbolizes industrial progress few questioned in the seventies. I work the car culture image through an actual encounter I had with a car salesman while exploring plug-in hybrid car options. The poem ends with a return to abundance, but of an organic type, with the lifting of a flock of curlews from a dried slough basin. My hope is that what lingers is the movement of birds.

FIX

Monica Kidd

Pumpjack legs spindle into
caked loam, steel heart
touch-warm. Kantian man's
sunset stride, ruggedly
backlit.

O, lonely miner
feasting on deep time.
Fueling 454s roaring up 21,
windows ringent,
punching up Desperado
on the eight-track.

That you

never

stopped

meant

we

were

the chosen.

Good old boy smells of last night.
Winks me toward his cubicle
with a glossy mag and business card.
Dear melancholy electron. How crude
tumescence weaponizes the fearful.

Stop the car. Step onto prairie ground
stoic with grasshopper drone.
Curlews flash from the salt pond,
tattoo an afterimage of wings.
Our pupils fix in surprise.

Look. How everything vanished.

Process images by Kasia Koralewska. Top to bottom: Soaking and cooking osage and logwood chips. Straining liquid dye and thickening with sodium alginate. Indigo pigment is mixed with soybean solution.

CYCLE
Screen print with natural dyes on raw silk (osage and logwood)
2022, 48.3 x 33 cm.

Kasia Koralewska

STATEMENT

I am a textile artist; my practice focuses on textile surface design through silkscreen printing. Recently, I dedicated my research to exploring natural dyes as my primary printing medium. It is a way to transform my practice into a more sustainable one. However, I am aware that it is not a solution. The issue of sustainability is very complex, and I am interested in discovering its layers. The Energy Futures project allows me to learn from fellow artists, writers and scientists and contribute to a positive climate change. The collaborative nature of Energy Futures is instrumental in developing my design. I have the pleasure of working with a writer and poet, Monika Kidd. After discussing our shared interests regarding renewable energy in Alberta, Monica has written a poem that inspired the imagery for my print. It was also important that parts of my design refer to the carbon sequestration process. Thinking about the potential of this process led me to the title I chose for my piece: Cycle. I found it crucial to produce the prints using materials appropriate for the topic of this project. I chose to work with natural dyes instead of synthetic ones—oil by-products. The dyes derived from nature can bind only with natural fibres, strongly favouring protein-based ones. Therefore, I chose to print on raw silk.

• • •

Kasia Koralewska is a textile-based artist and art educator currently living in Calgary, Canada. She received her education at the Alberta College of Art & Design in Calgary, Canada and Academy of Fine Arts in Lodz, Poland (Master of Fine Arts 2009). She presently teaches in the Fibre program at the Alberta University of the Arts. Her research focuses on exploring various techniques and processes used in textile surface design with a focus on sustainability.

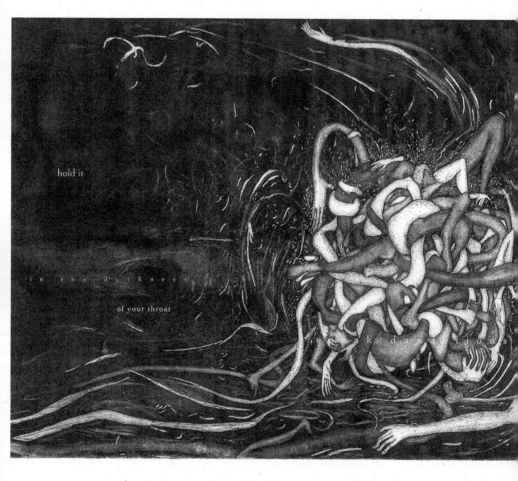

where to store hope (detail), Jamie-Lee Girodat.
Etching, silkscreen, and relief print. Text by Kim Mannix.
Artist's statement is at the end of this chapter.

CHAPTER FOUR

WHERE TO STORE HOPE

Kim Mannix, Author
Jamie-Lee Girodat, Artist

WHERE TO STORE HOPE

in caverns craving light

at the centre of a knot

where the shadow of one hand covers another

in the hollow of mother's collarbone

let it settle in the fissures of your skin

hold it
                   in the darkness

of your throat

speak dandelions

THOUGHTS ON MY
SELFISH JOURNEY TOWARD HOPE
Kim Mannix

"We've got room down there."

It was that simple statement, said by Candice Paton, Executive Director at Enhance Energy, during one of our many enlightening and inspiring information sessions for this project, that nudged open a door in my own mind. She was talking about carbon sequestration. A way, she said, to find a safe and secure home for something that harms the atmosphere. It brought to mind the very reasons so much of my poetry, both consciously and subconsciously, convenes at an intersection of climate concern, feminism, and motherhood. Why I often write to cope with grief and worry, and to remind myself how the earth, like my body and the bodies of all the women that came before me, can capture memories and store knowledge. How a body—of work, of humanity —can be a place to keep history and incubate change. It was a small push against something that seemed, in me, so stubbornly closed to hope.

Next came conversations with Jamie-Lee Girodat, an artist whose work also spoke to me in a way that seemed deeper than just admiration for her skill and talent. There was something organic, stirring, and familiar to me in her drawings and etchings. During our talks, we both expressed a need to find a reservoir for optimism and ingenuity. For a solution grander and more realistic than personal responsibility. How, cooperatively, using brains and hearts and hands, we can reach for what she called "a sense of care."

The more she described her vision, the more my words began to take shape in that fascinating and mysterious way that poems do. I was pushed to let my naturally negative brain wander deep into a secret creative space. One that can see an innovative, love-lit path instead of one that simply ends.

It seems to me that symbols, both the shorthand kind used in math and science to represent detailed concepts, and the metaphorical kind we weave into the fabric of our various modes of art-making, work in the most efficient of ways. The symbol that carried me to the end of this project was dandelions. Bright and resilient, they embody feminine energy. They insert themselves into spaces where they may not be wanted but could be needed. They grow en masse, a collective of yellow. I started reading more about them and discovered they can grow in tailings ponds and can even help to clean them. Dandelions transform in such effortless fashion. The air that feeds everything carries its seeds. They root, down there, where there is still room for hope, and they grow.

• • •

Kim Mannix writes poetry and prose on Treaty 6 territory in Sherwood Park, Alberta. She serves on the Edmonton Poetry Festival Board and is a member of the Writers' Guild of Alberta, The Edmonton Stroll of Poets, and the League of Canadian Poets. She's a contributing editor of Watch Your Head, *a climate crisis anthology, and works as an entertainment journalist.*

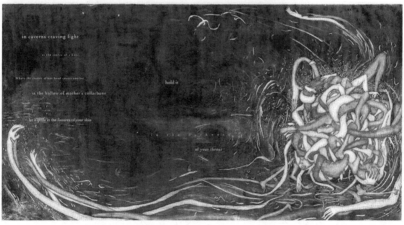

where to store hope (detail and full image),
Jamie-Lee Girodat. Etching, silkscreen, and relief print.

WHERE TO STORE HOPE
Etching, silkscreen, and relief, 2022. 48.3 x 91.4 cm.
Text by Kim Mannix

Jamie Lee-Girodat

STATEMENT

where to store hope unfolds to reveal a mass of arms tangled within the earth's shadows. Hands grip to protect bellies of the future, but also gently caress, exhibiting the soft malleability of the skin. Unravelling the knot would be a burdensome task. Yet there is lightness as fragments drift away, becoming rudiments of change. Collaboration, education, and responsibility are essential to Alberta's carbon sequestration development. As a province that excretes vast amounts of oil from the earth, it is necessary to reverse the damage we have done. Restoration requires sharing knowledge and building momentum for both the environmental and economic opportunities of the energy transition. Pining to dismantle constraints and fears, *where to store hope* attempts to enter a state of renewal and possibility. By combining Kim Mannix's poem with printed imagery, the work envisions a future that cares for the values of others and future generations.

• • •

Jamie-Lee Girodat resides in Mi'kma'ki (Sackville, NB) as a contract Assistant Professor at Mount Allison University. She considers Alberta home and has completed a BFA at the University of Lethbridge and an MFA in Printmaking at the University of Alberta. Genetic history, ethics, and misinformation in health guide her interdisciplinary practice which has been exhibited nationally and internationally.

Cycle of Healing, Jessica Semenoff. Screenprint.
Artist's statement is at the end of this chapter.

CHAPTER FIVE

REVERSING THE FLOW

Shannon Kernaghan, Author
Jessica Semenoff, Artist

REVERSING THE FLOW

after decades of industry expansion

deformed fish found in a lake downstream

from oil sands, whitefish with tumours big

as golf balls, good reasons for studies on the health

of the Athabasca River and its watershed

independent monitoring

after fear, many afraid to eat lake fish

from local anglers who know the bond

between fish health and human health

life of a community

it's time to reverse the flow

rejig current trajectories

nurture our ecosystem

refresh bonds

recreate legacies

after decades of industry expansion

SWEET AND CLEAR

She kneels at the coffee table
concentrates on her tablet, deep diving . . .
Mom, she says, this article is about Navajo tribal members
who graze their sheep in New Mexico.
Her volume increases: Mom! Their air smells
of rotten eggs and their water once came from a mountain
spring sweet and clear, now it runs yellow.
The people can drink bottled water but their sheep can't!
Drilling will destroy their simple lives!
Mom, this isn't right, where will these people go
when their land and air is too polluted?
I say nothing, several seconds
touch the back of her once corn-silk hair
now streaked a matte black, 16 going on 36.
My turn: maybe you can learn more
about how to make a difference,
take college courses after high school.
She rejects my suggestion
with her usual trifecta: snort + eye roll + wrist flap
but when she later leaves for the bathroom
I lean over to find her screen filled with
Environmental Management course material
and I feel more hopeful than I have for years.

OUTLAND

You sneak me into your camp room
hurry me through your plant
that resembles the Sean Connery movie set
Outland—
a remote mining colony on Jupiter's moon Io.
Bleak, unknown territory for this sub/urban girl.

You want me to know where you sleep
and work but could lose your job if we're caught
with racing hearts, holding hands
forged at the hip in our espionage
fast-stepping empty hallways
more like Sean Connery avoiding the enemy
than one grass widow who spends
too little time with her man, always away
always headed north.
Your film's third act is a drive past a tailings pond
and for a change I say nothing, only stare
otherworldly, out of my element
this outland.

SLIPPERY

A snapshot of my life:
Picture me riding my blue bicycle on the trails along
(aptly named) Black Gold Drive
pedalling beneath a QE2 overpass.
I stop, look up to watch semis roll north,
a parade of trucks that bloom pipes, spools
and pumpjacks to extract that black gold.
Fort McMurray, ground zero oil sands
where industries and tradespeople flock to the smell
of oil buried in sandy soil, soil made rich with dinosaur bones.
Still pedalling, an epiphany gushes up:
my life plays out like a movie and I am living a script,
uneasy as the actor I've been cast.
Some days I am Goodfellas Karen Hill
surrounded by mafia wives she can't relate to,
criminal actions she can't condone. But.
She won't walk away from the money until it's too late.
Will this be my fate when my partner's job is eliminated,
that we waited too long to leave as oil dips low,
reserves dance high?
Other days I am Matt Damon in Promised Land hired
by a natural gas corp to woo drilling rights.
Damon's character grows conflicted—rural folks nice,
company ethics sketchy, fracking risky.
"It's only a job," says his co-worker,
yet to the landowners, it's their lives and livelihoods.
Just like in Alberta, it's our lives and our livelihoods.
Read that however you like, as in cherished land

versus cherished oil industry jobs.

Now, pick a tarry side and try to stay on it.

Back to my snapshot:

At the end of Annie Hall, Woody Allen tells a joke.

Guy walks into a psychiatrist's office and says,

"Hey doc, my brother's crazy, he thinks he's a chicken."

Doc says, "Why don't you turn him in?"

Guy says, "I would but I need the eggs."

In my landscape, replace "eggs" with "oil"

and here I back pedal, feeling slippery because

love it, hate it, I'm connected to Oil Country,

caught in the nether region between utopia and dystopia

with a crystal ball hazed by fly ash.

All I can hope for is middle ground, environmentalists

and oil companies meeting half way before

I join the dinosaur bones.

May this oily story not end like the original Planet of the Apes.

The structure buried by sand won't be the Statue of Liberty's torch,

but the broken wheels of my blue bike.

Shannon Kernaghan writes and creates visual art from Alberta. Her poetry explores the lives of oil industry workers: what happens when their environmental protection side clashes with their need to make a living? Kernaghan is published in books, journals, and newspapers—poetry, essays, and everything between.

CYCLE OF HEALING.
Screenprint, 2022, 48.3 x 33 cm.

Jessica Semenoff

STATEMENT

The Athabasca oil sands, while providing jobs and economic growth, have a tremendously negative impact on the surrounding environment. Numerous fish have been found in the Athabasca River with deformities including crooked tails, lesions, tumours, and bulging eyes. The cause? Harsh toxins leach into the river directly downstream of the oil sands tailing ponds.

While my artwork was created specifically about the Athabasca River, it parallels other crude oil disasters. There have been similar deformed fish found in the Gulf of Mexico and the Gulf of Alaska after oil spill disasters.

As the fish depicted in my print pass through the barrel with oil, lesions begin to spread. Carrying on through the barrel absent with oil, they begin to heal. The image mirrors what would happen in the Athabasca River if the oil sands production halted, and pollutants were removed from the environment. When we allow mother nature to restore herself, the ecosystem doesn't take long to spring back to life.

• • •

Jessica Semenoff is a Calgary-based muralist, painter, and printmaker who gathers imagery and inspiration from flora and fauna. These ideas are then transferred to canvas and paper by means of paint and printmaking techniques. Her adoration for the environment has pushed her to begin incorporating themes of sustainability, climate change, and our flawed landfill and recycling.

Mendeleyev's Dream, Mary Kavanagh. Stack of cut acrylic sheets with periodic table of the elements. Below: Cut acrylic sheet superimposed on inkjet print on BFK Rives paper. Artist's statement is at the end of this chapter.

CHAPTER SIX

BUSTED

Donna Williams, Author
Mary Kavanagh, Artist

"Why Ontario, Troy?"

"It's where the work is." He stirs two teaspoons of sugar into his coffee. "You wait, Sonia, Alberta will have it, too, and I'll have a leg up."

"Why are you calling it the new nuclear? Whose slogan is that?" Sonia takes a bite of toast spread with last summer's saskatoon jam. Delicious. She pulls a chair to sit at the kitchen table.

"It's safer, for one."

"—if you believe that."

"I do." Troy is leaning against the counter, his arms crossed, either in defence or defiance. Likely both.

"There's still risk. New risks. What hasn't been imagined, or worse, imagined and disregarded. Because something will happen, Troy."

"Don't catastrophize, Sonia." His words hang in the kitchen like the wait for a final peal of thunder.

Sonia takes another bite of toast and looks past Troy, the glass of a bay window marked with fresh rain. "But you're talking what? Being away for months, a year? Have you forgotten we've got another grand-baby on the way?"

"I know. But this work, it's what I'm good at."

"I don't know, Troy. The way the whole oil and gas industry has treated you. 'Now we want you, now we don't.'" The dance of boom and bust.

She doesn't say that she's good at her job, too, that she isn't flying off to Ontario as she waits for the local ER to re-open.

"It's work. And I want the work."

"But why this job?"

"Sonia, it's what I do."

"Leading a team is what you do," she says. "And to lead, don't you have to trust? Do you trust this new nuclear?"

"I do." He lifts his mug, sucks air with the hot coffee as he swallows.

She leans over her plate of half-eaten toast, her elbows landing loud on the laminate. She looks at Troy, trying to absorb this word new. "I mean, what do you even know about nuclear?"

"I know enough. At the very least, it's another energy. A way for folks to keep living the way they're living."

"And should folks keep living the way they're living?"

"No, but yes. It's why it's called an energy transition."

"To what? Nuclear reactors in every city, every country and continent?"

Troy smiles. "Not overnight." He takes another sip.

Sonia ignores the smile. "That's so much risk." Exponential risk. "And what if uranium falls into the wrong hands?"

"That's the stuff of novels and you know it."

"But there's the threat of nuclear war, now! It's unnerving." Her mood darkens like a sky heavy with prairie hail.

She looks past him once more to the window now solid with rain. Troy installed the window after Sonia's mother died, the spring Sonia was the sort of sad that laid her too low to even lie down, the summer she sewed. In all this time, she cannot remember such rain. After a winter without snow, unless you count the stinging pellets that flew horizontal last fall, or the slush that melted in a day mid-January. The fields are thirsty. Maybe the land is asking for this rain that doesn't stop.

"Other countries are shutting them down," she adds.

"And others are ramping up."

She drops her chin on both fists and raises her face to Troy.

"There it is," he says with a grin, "You sure are pretty."

She knows he means the glint of gold, what he calls her party sequin, in the bottom quarter of her left iris. Alluring, he whispered when they first met—the planet's wealth of gold at the bottom of the ocean, and he gets a glint every single day.

"Oh, not now, Troy." She wants to punch him and bake him pie.

Troy empties his mug in a decisive chug and places it on the counter. "The reactors are smaller, transportable. And without nuclear, net zero is impossible. I believe that, too."

Watching Troy hook his thumbs in his belt loops, Sonia hears him say "industrial co-generation" and "high-quality heat" but is thinking of his prostate scare. Nuclear medicine is helpful, and radioisotopes treat tumours.

Sonia lifts a piece of toast only to set it back down. "What about the new waste? It's still radioactive. And for-ever."

"Not forever."

"It might as well be. We'll be long gone, our kids, their kids, their kids' kids, their kids' kids' kids—"

"I get it—" Troy sways despite leaning.

"It's what's hidden that gets forgotten. At least with fossil fuels, we see the waste."

"Exactly. The energy from nuclear is clean."

"But it's still capitalism at its core. Listen to yourself, Troy. You are a clichéd cog in this, whatever new nuclear wheel."

"Because that wheel? It drives our economy."

He releases his thumbs and reaches for Sonia's toast. What he doesn't say, what they both know, is that he needs something to do besides being out of work, alone with himself, his thoughts, day in and out.

"You gotta help me out here, Sonia. What choice do I have? Tell me that."

Sonia runs her hand through her hair, sees the time on the back of the stove and stands from the table. She grabs her empty plate and opens the dishwasher. Full. She drops the dish into the sink and looks at Troy.

"Troy, it's a bad idea."

ii ·

CKUA is playing "Wondering Where the Lions Are" as the Toyota rushes past fields shorn of wheat. Electrical posts fly past her window, seemingly as fast as the years have flown, too. All they hoped their lives would be.

Sonia's hands tighten on the steering wheel. How does he not see the sheer ominousness of nuclear? 'Don't catastrophize, Sonia?' It's because nuclear is not without incident. Meltdowns, radioactive fallout, deaths, cancers.

And to build those new ones, the small modular reactors, the SMRs? They're so expensive they need massive subsidies. Why didn't she think to say that to Troy?

The rain slows then stops. Sonia loosens her grip, then clicks off the wipers to a navy-grey vista dotted with low bulbous clouds. This sky, over this swatch of earth, has been with her nearly every day of her life. Today, it looks like a favourite, pilled sweater, but one she knows is suffocating the earth with its warmth.

Isn't it better to put the money toward renewables like wind and solar, that can be ready quickly?

The echo of 'You gotta help me, Sonia.'

Help you? Help me!

Her head-nurse job, the one she planned to retire from when the timing was right, disappeared with budget cuts. If the ER doesn't re-open soon, she'll resort to nightshifts. She doesn't rationalize whether the disruption to her sleep won't bother her if Troy goes, or if the money might be enough to keep him from going—it doesn't matter. He wants to work, she knows this. She releases one hand to rub the back of her left thigh, then adjusts the seat for her sciatica.

Sonia and Troy asked a neighbour what alternative fuel they supported, and their answer was: all of it. Better than the crazy (but real) idea Sonia read about—lowering the earth's temperature by injecting the sky with chemicals. How much could the atmosphere take?

Help me, Sonia.

How? Tell me that, Troy!

She slows for a curve in the road beside a land so striking her breath halts. A distant row of pines and old ryegrass glowing golden with the wet. How stable the land seems resting placidly on the other side of windshield. Yet, the opposite is true, predictably so—nothing as certain as change. Is Troy right? Are these new reactors the way forward? If the science is sound, why does it feel so wrong?

She wipes the grit from the dashboard, and thinks, what used to be stardust is now satellite dust too.

iii

Gini's Barber Shop is oddly empty when Sonia pushes open the door. Frugality led her here the first time Troy was laid off, her thick hair forever in need of a trim. But the chair brought an unexpected gift in the form of Gini. A woman who meets angst or anguish with belief: whose nodding head means Uh huh, that's hard, an empathy of I-will-walk-with-you and laugh-with-the-unfairness, even if I don't-know-your-darkness. Her chair holds the meditative cure of a walk amongst aspens, but with efficiency. A good quick cut in a restorative fifteen minutes, or, if it is Sonia, a bit longer.

"So?" asks Gini.

Sonia sees her reflection in the mirror. Her gold eye-freckle is still inflamed after the fight with Troy.

"Troy."

A nod.

"He gets a notion and without any deliberation whatsoever, BOOM! It's reality." Sonia knows this isn't quite true. Troy speaks only when he's thought something through. Annoying, because she likes all options on the kitchen table for sorting.

"I mean, have you ever heard of a thorium molten salt reactor?"

"I have," Gini replies. "The smaller ones, modular."

"Yes! Troy–"

"Expensive, but the same problem, all that spent fuel. The new idea for a burial site half-a-kilometre underground is appalling."

"Exactly, out of sight, out of–"

"Mind? More like out of their minds. Not a good idea." She raises both eyebrows at Sonia. "Cracking open the earth for uranium, leaching it free? Tailings ponds and the transport of yellow cake–"

Talking about energy in Alberta is as common as talking about the weather, but usually it's Gini listening to Sonia. Today, there's an agitation in Gini and Sonia knows what it means. Shifting her thoughts away from Troy, she asks softly, "How's your mom doing?"

"This morning I popped over on my way to the shop. She offered me toast, and the whole loaf of bread was mouldy. I asked how old it was. She snapped, 'I just bought it. Do you think I'd poison you?' The best-before was two months ago, Sonia."

Gini stops cutting, "I said, 'Mom, you're worrying me, and she slammed the fridge door and told me to get out."

Sonia looks at Gini in the mirror, Gini, holding scissors in her hand, staring at Sonia.

"She's all I can think about—it's like she's walking on crusted snow with no worry about crashing through. I'm the one feeling buried. I'm forgetting to listen to messages, so I have no idea who wants appointments. How am I going to care for her? My own house, Beth in high school?"

Gini pulls thinning shears through Sonia's hair, suddenly silenced by her own thoughts. Sonia considers what to say—she can see her own mother's half-cup of coffee lit by the light of the sewing machine where she made wedding dresses and smoked cigarettes, both at the same time. Sewing all night.

She hears Troy's voice, 'What are you afraid of?' What is she afraid of? Gini's fears are immediate—all that's between now and losing her mom. Sonia's fears are theoretical, and she's mad at Troy for not seeing them, too.

Gini turns to answer a buzzing phone, leaving Sonia to calculate how to extend her time in town without spending money. She pictures Troy at home, rototilling the garden in preparation for the May long weekend. If he goes to Ontario, he won't be around for planting.

"You want a blow dry? I have time." Gini is back and nodding to the empty chairs. Sonia is used to leaving with damp hair, even at minus twenty.

It seems wrong to take more from Gini, yet Sonia says, "Sure."

"You heading away this summer?" Gini's voice is artificial over the drone of the hair dryer.

Sonia hesitates, caught with the realization that nuclear will go ahead, with or without Troy. She realizes, too, that Troy has decided.

Oh, to wish for the years when she and Troy were busy becoming themselves, when they were energetic and moving forward with a recklessness, because why not? But the danger of nostalgia are memories more glorious than their reality. The golden years are meant to be ahead.

"He's taking a job in Ontario," she answers. The words taste bitter, and she swallows.

Gini might have asked, "What about you? What will you do?" Or sighed, "Of course—you'll miss him."

But instead, she places the hair dryer in its holder and unfastens the cape. As she sweeps the hair trimmings into the garbage, Sonia thinks of what Gini said about storing nuclear waste half-a-kilometre underground. What a dreadful legacy to leave behind.

Gini walks to the front and waits to pass Sonia the debit machine. Sonia finds her card and taps, handing back the machine, only Gini is standing, unmoving, staring at her hands as if they belong to someone else.

iv

On the table, LIST is written in Troy's hand across a piece of paper; Sonia is unsure whether it's for groceries, or for packing. Troy is washing the dirt from his hands at the kitchen sink—the scent of Sunlight reaches Sonia, and she smiles.

He looks over his shoulder. "Maybe call nuclear something else. Something friendlier."

"That's hardly the point, Troy." But maybe that's the plan, a nuanced name for nuclear to make it palatable. She sits and picks up a pencil, jots new nuclear. Then nuance. Nuanced Energy. NuancE. She could make a buck or two in marketing.

NuClear. NuDay. NuWay.

"What's the old nuclear to the next generation anyway?" he adds, drying his hands on a tea towel meant for dishes—Sonia long since stopped asking him to use the hand towel.

"You don't mean that," she says. No way. She draws a couple of vertical lines rising into an exploding cloud, then lays the pencil down. ·

He glances at her drawing, opens his mouth, only to close it. Their eyes move to the seed packets she brought home earlier from the hardware store, resting on the table like postcards from their future garden. Beets, carrots, scarlet runner beans.

Troy turns and opens the fridge, removes an enameled roaster with last night's chicken. "Nuclear puts us on track to phase out coal, even natural gas. And it's a good fit for the oil sands." What she hears in his voice is resignation—it's a good fit for him. Despite her objections of 'Troy, it's a bad idea,' he is moving forward.

Sonia stands and leans into the window, the evening sun slung low amongst mottled clouds. A magpie swoops deep and is away. This window frames her dreams, keeps her life simple. The show of a yellow sky foretelling a winter storm, or a clear star-scape bringing down the summer heat. She was born in this house. The small square of land resting out the window is now hers, a bit of income. Is she supposed to pack up? Start over?

Nothing like the stare of a prairie dusk with no answers, but welcoming questions.

She moves to drain a pot of steaming beets in the sink, running the cold tap as she starts to slip away their skins, the water turning scarlet.

"You just have to trust," Troy says.

"Trust who? You, or our government, or the new nuclear? Who should I trust?" She looks over to see him slice into the breast and tear off one remaining leg, dividing the meat between two plates.

"Because you and me, Troy? We're not the problem. We're not flying off to Mexico every five minutes." They'd been composting before composting was composting. And with Troy's green thumb —no pesticides. They'd put extra insulation in the attic years ago. They're not the problem.

But she knows this is wrong. All their actions accumulate in the bigger world. She watches Troy remove the wishbone and place it in the bay window to dry.

Sonia finishes the beets, dries her hands on the same tea towel as Troy, her fingers tinted red. She watches as Troy spreads a knob of butter across the smooth, still-steaming beets. Despite her concern over their cholesterol levels, Troy has a point; can't she simply enjoy the taste?

Troy sees Sonia watching and lifts one shoulder, a half-shrug. "I'm optimistic, that's all."

Sonia holds his eyes, says, "You are hopeful."

"I am."

Wasn't she hopeful, too? Or did she really believe the world was beyond care? If she did, she would be more generous to Troy, and to herself. Because then, what did it matter? Maybe they would fly off to Mexico. Instead, she feels robbed of day-to-day joys. Flinging herself into tomorrow in an overwhelm of worry. And yet, isn't tomorrow still for deciding?

What she wants to say brings tears slipping down her throat. That she'll miss him. Miss his warmth each night, their backs to each other, their feet touching—hers with the beginnings of bunions, his wide and surprisingly soft.

She runs her hand along the softness of her neck to the fresh feel of her haircut. Slowly, she starts to tell him about Gini.

• • •

Donna Williams is a Calgary-based writer and a born and raised Albertan. She writes eco-fiction and is proud to be a part of this important collection. She believes the current moment in climate crisis is knowable through fiction, with characters who intrigue, shock, and ultimately enter our hearts. She holds a Master's degree in English literature.

Mendeleyev's Dream, Mary Kavanagh.
Original notes on periodic table by Dimitri Mendeleyev (1867).
Below: cut acrylic sheet.

MENDELEYEV'S DREAM
Cut acrylic sheet; Inkjet print on BFK Rives paper, 2022,
33 x 48.3 cm each.

Mary Kavanagh

STATEMENT

In 1869 Dmitri Mendeleyev, a Russian chemist and teacher, advanced the bold hypothesis of elemental periodicity, claiming it came to him in a dream. After days of feverishly labouring to solve the riddle of the classification of the chemical elements, until then clouded in alchemy and mystery, he awoke with a vision and quickly jotted down the figures and columns that became the foundation of the modern periodic table. One hundred and eighteen elements now complete the table, a tidy summation of matter, organized into metals, non-metals, lanthanides, actinides, metalloids, halogens, and noble gases. That this finite, codified list represents all matter, the contents of which combine into all the substances in the universe with neither loss nor gain, is a confounding concept, and one that has captivated me while working on this project. Envisioning energy began with looking straight up, pointing my camera at the sky. Rayleigh scattering of sunlight into sublime blues and changing hues gave way to the contested skies of surveillance, orbiting satellites, warfare, bombing raids, terror. Terror from the air—especially in an era in which the main target of warfare is the environment, or the very conditions necessary to sustain life—is intimately tied to energy futures. By superimposing a transparent grid of the periodic table onto a photograph of clouds adrift without end, these images are bound together, the contained and the uncontainable, the known and the unknowable.

• • •

Mary Kavanagh is an artist and professor in the Department of Art at the University of Lethbridge. She is a Board of Governors Research Chair awarded for her work examining the material evidence of war, translated through moving image, photographic, archival and spatial practices. Kavanagh's work is exhibited across Canada and internationally. She is a Fellow of the Royal Society of Canada, Academy of Arts and Humanities.

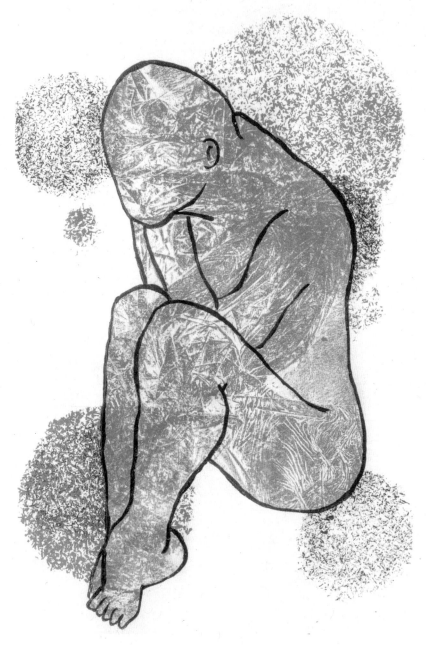

Clingwrap, Jacqueline Huskisson.
Collagraph and mixed media.
Artist's statement is at the end of this chapter.

CHAPTER SEVEN

CLING WRAP

Natalie Meisner, Author
Jacqueline Huskisson, Artist

CLING WRAP

Eighty years of lovingly wrapping
everything in clear plastic
& we are less transparent to ourselves
than ever
piled high & deep in
a thin veneer of polyvinylidene chloride
which sounds musical if you say it out loud
unless you know what it is

As a child if anyone threw garbage
out the window I took it as personally
as if they'd thrown it in my face
& acted accordingly

I got in a lot of fistfights
until the aunties warned me
I would have to learn to live
in the world as it is

You think it's bad now, they said
later on you will know more
if you live long enough
you will enter an age of rage
& it will come like a brutal wave, you'll see
you'll be standing on the ramparts
yelling as you are now
but people will hear you less and less

It will be as if you speak through
a layer of invisible wrapping
the indestructible puzzles of today
gifted to humans of the future wrapped
in a thin shimmering coating,
of polymer chains, so thin so indestructible
we barely see them in the water
yet they catch at us when we want to swim.

Our take out containers, our bread ties
our tiny plastic soldiers & our forks and knives.
Our medical waste & our bags bags bags
sing a hymn to laziness and sloth.
We try to swim away clean to the breakwater
but thin shimmering chains foul our fins
cling to every limb & appendage
the seas are stogged, our third eyes clogged
filmy & cataracted with cling wrap.

In the grocery aisle I think of the aunties
& hoist a cucumber aloft: the new Excalibur
& howl why is the perfect
emerald green wrapping
of this sacred vegetable
that it grew for itself sheathed
in five layers of transparent death?

What are we trying to wrap up & save, & from what?
The air, the water the heat the sun, ourselves?
We've already made synthetic rope enough
to hang ourselves & every other creature
yet we go on weaving
more rope does not help
like rage does not help
nor does hope, alone
yet my ear is keen and tuned

It is happening, my aunties, rumbling
& coming from some rooted some ancient place
the inchoate howl
the wordless song of all that's wrong

MADE TO BREAK
(A LOVE POEM TO THE OBJECT IN MY HAND)

Planned obsolescence
is just a fancy way of saying
I love you
or loved you, rather
briefly but thoroughly
with an acquisitive passion
so immediate, so lizard brain
I could not keep my hands off you.

Sleek, shiny, enigmatic
I stroked your contours
gazed into your inky obsidian depths
a composite of all faces
all knowledge & consciousness
desiring & knowing I could never fully know
all you hold inside
your circuitry merged with mine,
our synopsis' glowed up warm belly fire.

In thrall I plunged into you
head first, ass sticking up
as a bee lunges into the heart of a flower—
though you're killing the bees
can you please stop
killing all the bees?
I mainlined pollen plunged into
the sticky limbic morass of pleasure
searching for the place where wires
& blood vessels entwine

In thrall of all you promised
to teach me, I picked you up
& brought you home
gave you pride of place
in my hand, pocket & bed

In the dark I made offerings to you
found love in this loveless age
trusted you with my secrets but now—
how could you?
you are broken & refuse to do the things
you used to do
you've never wake me up
or tuck me in
you won't fire up &
only let me down, reflecting back
the harsh mask of my own
disappointed human face.

What choice do I have?
but to send you to landfill
with all the others to be piled & sifted
split open & smashed & eventually
boiled down in open vats
by small children who stir
& breathe your last chemical gasps
because you were made
yes made to break.

But what can I do?
We humans so fond of
narratives that lean into
helplessness
It's not my fault,
It's bigger than me,
It's baked into
the system,
the system you can't fight
the system we're born into
& the system is a thing it is slowly becoming clear
like you, like me,
all human animals & machines we are
made to break

• • •

Natalie Meisner is a playwright and poet hailing from Nova Scotia.
She is a full Professor at Mount Royal University and Calgary's 5th Poet
Laureate. Her work deploys the power of comedy for social change.
Titles include: Baddie One Shoe, Legislating Love: The Everett
Klippert Story, Speed Dating For Sperm Donors, Double Pregnant:
Two Lesbians Make a Family, My Mommy, My Mama, My Brother &
Me, *and* It Begins in Salt.

CLING WRAP
Mixed media: acrylic paints on various papers, collagraph made from Saran Wrap and artificial grass. 2022. 48.3 x 33 cm.

Jacqueline Huskisson

STATEMENT

I aim to create an impression, a lasting reflection of an abstract emotion in the viewer, and a reflection on their place in the universe. I do this by surrounding the viewer with my art, engulfing them with media such as wallpaper, murals, and engrossing comics. I am interested in exploring the line between reality and fiction and creating my own interpretation of where that line is. My artworks are ultimately questions to viewers about their perceptions of modern life, the human condition, and an active study of my own personal situation. I printed a collagraph from Saran Wrap (cling-wrap) on Mulberry paper, which I cut into a human form. I pasted this shape with poly acrylic medium onto another collagraph print made from fake grass. The final form is outlined by hand with acrylic paint. I intentionally avoided buying new materials and reused what I had on hand.

• • •

Jacqueline Huskisson received a BFA in Print Media from AU Arts in 2011. In 2017 she received an MFA in Interdisciplinary Studies from the Belfast School of Art. She has had solo exhibitions at Alberta Printmakers, Poolside Gallery, Lowlands Projects Space, and most recently with the Helmut project space in Leipzig, Germany. Jacqueline has also been doing various projects, installations, and residencies around Canada, the US, and Europe. She is the recipient of various local and national grants and was the inaugural recipient of the Scott Leroux Media Arts Exploration Fund and received a Juror's award for SSNAP 2021.

More Than Patchwork, Nadia Perna.
Digital Print on archival paper.
Artist's statement is at the end of this chapter.

CHAPTER EIGHT

DEAR ALFAH

Barb Howard, Author
Nadia Perna, Artist

Dear Alfah,

I was wondering today if you've ever received a letter, like this, on actual paper. I haven't sent a physical letter in over a decade. Not even a crummy card, bought at the pharmacy, that I slapped my signature on. But today I am feeling nostalgic, so paper it is.

Your mom tells me you are headed to the mountains at the end of the month. A hike in Banff with friends, she says. That got me thinking about the mountain trips I used to go on. And maybe I still would, even though I'm ancient, if it wasn't such a hassle. I hear that now we're all supposed to take the new hydrogen train, the H-train, to get to the mountains. The hassle train, as I think of it. What sort of way is that to start a happy day of outdoor recreation, jammed in like market pigs? Sorry, I know you're a vegetarian.

Some of us still eat bacon, or Wilbur or Miss Piggy or Babe, as you variously call it as I am eating. I used to eat even more bacon. One time after skiing I had a bourbon bacon cocktail — complete with a bacon "stir stick" the size of a one-foot ruler. Those were the days. Guilt-free bacon and imperial measurement. Alright, the imperial measurement system made no sense. Be thankful you missed it. I don't know why we stuck with it for so long.

And, alright again, you won't be ordering a cocktail of any sort on the green H-train. You probably have to bring your own water. I heard from my friend June—she's the one always going for the Earth Mother vibe in her floor-length kaftans and hemp jewellery, last time you saw her she was selling honey in the lobby of my building—anyway, June said that her neighbour's friend's son said that the H-train schedule to Banff doesn't suit anyone's trip plans. I guess you know this since your mom tells me you've used it on several occasions—although she says you find it convenient. Still, you can borrow my car to get to your hike if you want. My car's electric, as you know. I'm not that far behind the times. But with the new private vehicle quotas in the parks, it's like they don't want Albertans to own a car at all. Good luck with that, I say. To paraphrase a famous saying from a time when I was your age, they'll have to pry the steering wheel of my car from my cold dead hands. My electric car, mind you.

I admit the electric car runs well. No more oil changes—I always felt those recommended intervals were rigged. Did my car really need an oil change that often? But I do miss the sound of an internal combustion engine. That vroom made me feel like I was really driving. With only electric vehicles on the road now, I wonder what will become of the word vroom? If you do take my car, I recommend the coffee place at the Bearspaw First Nation's new Travel Centre. I've charged there before. The Travel Centre has a single-origin Arabica dark roast. Ethically grown. Of course, in the way-old days we didn't even know there were different kinds of coffee. Coffee was coffee. And most of it was awful, but we didn't know it was awful.

When I die I'm leaving you my electric car. I know, I know, you say you don't want or need a car. But I worry that, stuck on a train, you will never experience the joy of steering your own way from Calgary to Banff, through that beautiful prairie-to-foothills-to-mountain route, like the landscape symbolized on the Alberta Shield, which is on the Alberta provincial flag and Coat of Arms. Well, alright, I can hear you saying there's no highway pictured on that symbol. But you know what I mean. When I was younger than you are now, I'd drive to Banff in my diesel hatchback with the cassette blaring Joe Walsh's "Life's Been Good." The original version of that song is almost nine minutes long, pretty indulgent, but I guess that was the point. I'd be listening to Joe and I'd have the stick shift in one hand, an open mug of (bad) coffee in one hand, a cigarette going in the other hand—wait that's three hands—plus one hand on the steering wheel. Four hands! I don't know how I did it all. The smoking might surprise you. You probably didn't know that I was a smoker when I was your age. I loved smoking. If it didn't stink so much, and cloud up the air, oh, and kill people, I'd still smoke.

Speaking of smoke, I hope no one in your protest group is using smoke bombs. Even the police don't use those anymore. I don't suppose there is a green smoke bomb. Yet. Your mom tells me that you've been part of the continuing protests at the front doors of EMco. She says the situation is "heating up" and she's worried about your safety. And she's also worried that being part of such a group could damage your future. Well, she might not have said that last part but, as her much older sister, a full decade between us, I know that's what she was thinking (even if she doesn't know that's what she was thinking). Activism is fine in your 20s. When I was in my 20s I refused to pay my parking tickets and then sued the parking company for towing my car. There was never enough parking. I lost, but I had gumption. You come from a long line of gumption. But you don't want to make yourself unemployable. Who knows, you might need a job at EMco some day. I fully get the problem with emissions (remember, I have an electric car), and I appreciate the progress that has been made thanks to young people like you, but I think it would be best if you, Alfah, let the regulators handle EMco. There are rules and penalties for emissions. Why not have faith in them?

And don't forget that the oil patch, emissions and all, kept three generations of your family in a fine lifestyle. Your great-grandma was an investor, retired early after making a bundle off Imperial's Leduc No 1. Your grandma had a solid early retirement from Dome Petroleum in the 1970s (she got out before the skid). And your mother and me, as you know, were in the petrochemical business. If you're wearing nylon, polyester, spandex, elastane, viscose, or rayon on your hiking trip —thank us! Technical moisture-wicking clothing, that's me and your mom. We're darn proud of it. And we got to retire early, too! I recommend retiring early, although it seems not as common these days. It was an oilpatch perk.

Have the best of hiking trips. It should be cooler in the mountains. Once the temperature here in the city drops, maybe in a day or two, I'll walk this letter to the mail centre — while marvelling how, with all the changes in the world, Canada Post is still around.

xo Auntie

———

Dear Alfah,

Two weeks on and it's still too hot outside to take my last letter to the mail centre, so I'll just keep writing. You're probably already back from your hiking trip. I hope to see you sometime so you can tell me all about it.

While you were away your mom and I went for lunch at that overpriced deli, the one with the weird smell (I hear you saying it's the smell of meat, nice try but it's probably malt vinegar and disinfectant) and she told me that you are going in another march for climate change. Hard to believe marches are still a thing. Power to the people. Very 1960s. (Or that's what people nostalgic about the 1960s would have you think. I was a little kid in the 1960s and can tell you I had no power at all.) But marching is probably safer than hanging out at the front doors of EMco. Still, you've been going in marches since you were a teenager. The successes now are incremental. Maybe, at your age, you should focus on yourself? Take up a new sport?

How about pickleball? Or, for winter, how about downhill skiing? The carbon offset on the ticket certainly hasn't made it
cheaper. But, hey, it's all about the fun. I always had so much
fun downhill skiing. Maybe learn to teach skiing? I hear that's
one way to get around the mountain quota system in the winter. And, bonus, a way to cut through the lift lines, now that so
many tourists are coming from the south for our snow.

As for the climate change march, I get what it's like to
be pressured into doing things by friends. My friend June
—yes, earthy June—persuaded me to go to a quilt-making
course with her. I've known June for pretty much my whole
life, longer even than I've known your mother, so you'd think
she'd know that I hate crafts. But she came over to my place,
on the pretense of dropping off some soup that looked like
swamp water but tasted okay, and wouldn't leave until I agreed
to the quilting course. What else am I doing? Sitting at home
because of the heat, that's what, and reading article after article
about how old folks like me are the weaklings in heat domes.
I'm turning into a sad mope. On the upside, thank you again
for helping me move into this building last year. Who knew
the geothermal place would be cool in the summer? Well, I
guess you did. (And I guess you'd rather I call the technology
"ground source heat pump." But I won't. Everyone says geothermal.) It's like air conditioning, but better. I do sometimes
look out my window at the drooping trees and the sweltering
sidewalk and remind myself that even though I am trapped
inside, I'm lucky, I'm cool.

The only problem, and, alright, I recognize that it's more
of an inconvenience than a problem, is that because this building doesn't use natural gas my little fireplace here doesn't have
a log lighter. In my previous place I used to just turn on the gas
under the logs (real wood, but no kindling required), light a
match and, voila, the wood started on fire. You might ask who
needs an indoor fire in a heat dome? Fair enough, but we'll
see in winter. I know you said something about making me
fire-starter cubes. I'm guessing you mean the woodchip kind

and not the hydrocarbon paraffin kind. Either way, the cubes seem like more work than turning on the gas. I do know how to start a fire from scratch. When I was a kid we used to have massive bonfires. The bigger the better. We'd throw aerosol cans into the flames and kaboom! The kaboom isn't why they don't make that kind of aerosols anymore. They stopped making them because they were destroying the ozone layer. No one missed them.

Anyway, back to my friend June, I went to the quilting course with her. It's in the common room in my building so it will be cool. That might even be why June wants to take the course. I get it. I'm not interested in walking to a different location and, midway, trying to revive myself in a cooling centre (and for my age they say that doesn't always work.) The instructor wanted our money upfront, and everyone but June and I had paid, and so I felt pressured and I paid and committed to 12 long weeks of quilting class. I paid for June, too. That's how we roll. Her career wasn't in the oil patch.

I'm cranky with June for getting me into the quilting class. I'd rather just buy a quilt. But it does give me something to do. I'm working on a design that will have the Alberta Shield on it — it's been on my mind since I mentioned it in my earlier unmailed letter. June, who is working on a tree pattern, just triangles really, says my design is too ambitious. Start with something basic, she says. The instructor agrees with her. I say, why be basic when you can be ambitious? Right at this moment, as I write, I've decided to not only do the Alberta Shield but to also do a flying geese pattern for the border. To June and the instructor, I say honk honk.

When your mom and I were at the deli (I had a Reuben even though I don't like them much anymore and I don't know why I keep ordering them), she told me that, after the climate march, you are going on another trip with your friends. A bike trip to the Mînî Thnî Trail Park in the foothills now that the temperature has started dropping a bit. You'll be in good shape with all the bicycle commuting you do to your job. (Don't worry, I'm not going to ask you to explain your job to me again.) The Mînî Thnî Trail Park has terrific reviews, although the wind farm probably mucks up the eastern horizon. I've never been to that trail park, and I don't know anything about designing trail parks, but surely it's hard to keep wind turbines out of sight, even at that distance.

And your mom tells me that you are going on this trip with friends you met while bicycle commuting. Doesn't anyone use a car these days? Driving certainly is easier and faster than biking all the way to Mînî Thnî from Calgary, as your mom tells me you are planning to do. Even with the Westward Bike Pathway finally finished, it's a shame to take all the time to bike to the trailhead when, at least back in my day, the quality biking starts at the trailhead. A woman in my quilting class (not June, she stopped speaking to me after the third class) told me that her new husband's stepsister's daughter said that the Westward Bike Pathway is a massive failure that no one uses. So much money wasted on routing cyclists along the same corridor as the highway. Even though your mom said you like the Westward Bike Path for its shade and because it's not right beside the highway, why not drive? You can borrow my car if you want. It's electric.

I'm not going anywhere. Still too hot for this "vulnerable senior." I'm staying home and ruining my life by working on this quilt. I've cut up pieces from my old outdoor recreation clothing to create the Alberta Shield. For the sky, my blue polyester-spandex hiking tights from the 2020s. For the wheat, my yellow microfleece jacket, except for the parts held together with duct tape. And for the grasslands, my green acrylic toque. So much technical sweat-wicking material! I look at the colours laid out in front of me and realize that, back in the days of my outdoor prime, I must have looked like a petrochemical easter egg.

Everyone else in the class is almost finished their quilt tops. I guess they don't have anything going on in their lives either.

Or possibly they like quilting. And they're all patting each other on the back and virtue signalling about how much they did by hand. Not me. This building I'm living in has steady solar-generated electricity and I'm going to use my sewing machine. Vrooom, I say when I'm stepping on the machine's foot pedal. Take that, quilting class. Vroom.

The reason my friend June and I aren't speaking? I gave her a bit of friendly advice on the quilt she's making. She's using patches cut from her old batik kaftans. I said I've never seen a batik fir tree. Aren't fir trees green? She rolled her eyes at my Alberta Shield, and said that she'd never found that the Alberta landscape stunk like old sports clothing. I said it's not stinky, it's wick wear. She said, it stinks. And then we stopped talking. Alfah, between you and me, I bet June's quilt is going to stink of sage. She's been soaking herself in that scent her whole life. She smells like a bowl of Thanksgiving stuffing.

And about that coffee that I wrote about, and recommended, earlier — now I see an article in my unwanted newsfeed that coffee is never ethical. So you don't need to tell me that I shouldn't drink coffee. I've got too many people telling me what not to do. No one is ever going to take my coffee away from me. Ever. They're going to have to take my coffee mug from my cold dead hands.

I'll mail this when the temperature drops enough that I can walk to the mail centre. There's my electric car, of course, but it seems a shame to drive a distance that should be walkable. And, alright, it's not a significant enough trip to risk losing the perfect parking spot I have on the street, right below my window where I can check on my car whenever I want.

Have a great biking trip!

xo Auntie

———

Dear Alfah,

You're a sweet niece, but also a coy one. Showing up here on the first cool day in months and asking me to go for a walk along the river... and tricking me into a little canoe trip down the Bow. I would have said yes if you'd just asked me to go canoeing. Well, you might have had to waste some time convincing me. But I'm sure I would have come around to the idea.

You still had me fooled when we were walking to the river. I thought we were just going for a walk. But then I saw the gear library. How long has that been there? They even had the kind of beavertail paddle I favoured back in my paddling days. Now, I don't for a second believe the gear we borrowed was free. How could that be? So, tell me, how much do I owe you?

Alfah, I loved our trip down the river. By spending so much time inside I've been missing the river sounds, the gurgles and pops of water over rocks. The shore birds. Back in my paddling days there were often plastic bags on the shoreline and plastic bottles circling in the eddies — I'm glad we didn't see any of that.

And even though there will never be anything comparable to my old plastic Royalite canoe — that boat could bend around a rock and spring back into shape faster than a pair of petrochemical Spanx underwear (yes, Spanx were a thing) — the birchbark canoe we borrowed from the gear library has merits. I sold my Royalite because I didn't have room to keep it anymore and I wasn't using it, but I am sure that guy I sold it to is still using it. He got a deal. That canoe will be bobbing in the water 500 years from now. A birchbark canoe would be compost by then. But there is something to be said about paddling down the Bow in a birchbark canoe. It was a warm, quiet boat, beautiful inside and out.

I'm sorry I was bossy and giving too many instructions from the front of the boat. You are a superb paddler. It's been a long time since I've done an outdoor activity like that. I might have been nervous. Good nervous.

Alfah, even the electric shuttle van back to the put-in was a pleasant surprise. And the people who had borrowed canoes or used their
own for the river trip seemed nice. I mean, we could have used my
car for that part. It's electric, too. And has a rack. But the shuttle
was comfortable. The driver played a remixed version of Joe Walsh's
"Life's Been Good" which was perhaps (and here I feel downright
blasphemous) an improvement on the original.

I'm going to listen to Joe and some other artists from the 80s
(really the best decade of music since the beginning of time) as soon
as I finish this letter, and get to work on the quilt. I'm using an old
sleeping bag liner for the back. It looks a bit rough. June said it was
pilling (yes, we're talking again, we don't have enough time left in
our lives to stay bullheaded), but that's the side that no one will see.
Hopefully. On the upside, or should I say the frontside, the flying
geese were easy. Honk honk.

Last thing, thank you for the wild rosehip tea that you bought in
Mînî Thnî. I'm a coffee drinker. But maybe I'll try some of the tea if I
run out of coffee. Which is not to diminish the gift in any way. I was
so excited to see you in person that I forgot to hand you the letters
I've been writing you. The mail centre remains on my to-do list.

xo Auntie

———

Dear Alfah,

I ran out of coffee this morning and so I gave the rosehip tea
a try. Not bad at all. I'm not saying I am going to transition to it.
Yet. I haven't been able to get out to buy coffee, even though the
temperature is tolerable, because I am on a mission to finish this
Alberta Shield quilt. In case you haven't guessed, it's for you. That's
the thing with quilts—generally, they are for gifting. Or so my quilting classmates tell me. We're all still meeting even though the class
is over. New friends. That was unexpected. Life's been good to me.

June gave her batik-tree quilt to a hospice. Her quilt looked fabu-
lous, almost alive, with a border of tiny birds and flowers, all perfect

as though she made intricate woodsy quilts all the time. Her eyes were teary when she showed it to me, and I asked if she had cataract surgery or something. She said no they'd been teary for decades and I just never noticed. I don't know about that. It's like she was melting from her eyeballs. Pretty sure I would have noticed.

I plan to finish my quilt this weekend. I have the binding around the edges to do. And I'm embroidering, by hand, which isn't as bad as I thought, a fabric label for the back that says my name and the date. Oh, and the name of the quilt. I'm calling it Dear Alfah.

I'll package the quilt and the letters together and mail them Monday. The temperature looks normal, old normal, and the quilt is light, so I can walk the full distance to the mail centre. The quilt, alright, doesn't look as good as I envisioned. Not even close. But maybe you'll get out your scissors and a needle and some cotton thread and make this quilt your own. Make it better. Please.

xo Auntie

• • •

Barb Howard has published four novels, most recently Happy Sands, *and the story collection* Western Taxidermy. *A recipient of the Howard O'Hagan Award for Short Fiction and the Canadian Authors Association's Exporting Alberta Award, Barb has been a finalist at the Alberta Book Awards, Western Magazine Awards, and High Plains Book Awards, and has been published in periodicals across Canada.*

More Than Patchwork—elements, Nadia Perna. Digital image.

MORE THAN PATCHWORK
Digital Print on archival paper, 2022, 48.3 x 33 cm.

Nadia Perna

STATEMENT

More Than Patchwork explores intersectionality and a global just transition. Solving the climate crisis will require a collective transition to a system that values people and the planet over power and profit. The technological aspects of an energy transition are essential, but they are only one piece of the current patchwork approach. Instead of focusing on individual elements of the energy transition, *More Than Patchwork* considers a future where extraction and exploitation are replaced by conservation and equality. A just energy transition must be all-encompassing and inclusive. Developed in part through an artist-writer partnership with Barb Howard, the idea of quilting as a visual representation of a patchwork approach and clinging to the past is released into an organic state of flux. Energy transition will only matter if intersectionality is at its forefront, and a just future is created for all.

• • •

Nadia Perna is a designer, writer, and activist living in Mohkinstsis (Calgary). She graduated Alberta University for the Arts in spring 2023, with a Bachelor of Design with a major in graphic design and a minor in object design. She is an organizer with Fridays for Future Calgary, a youth-run climate justice organization. Her work, both in activism and design, centres around ideas of the intersectionality of a just transition and the role of empathy in designing a better future.

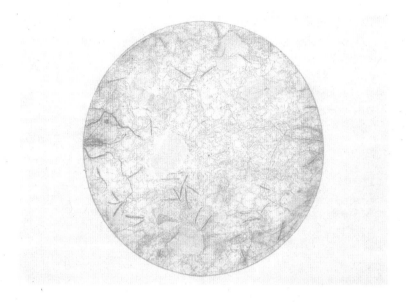

Top to bottom: *Under the Lens* and *Florence MA.*, Kate Baillies.
Intaglio on Kitikata paper.
Artist's statement is at the end of this chapter.

CHAPTER NINE

AND IT BURSTS WITH LIGHT

Richard Harrison, Author
Kate Baillies, Artist

OF ALBERTA LET US MAKE

There are days when working to repair the earth
seems hopeless. Climate change too far gone,
ice in retreat, forests burned by fires so predictable,
after them, we named a season.

There are days when selfishness seems
the sanest philosophy
and 24 hours
the right amount of future for which to plan.

On those days, I think of the cathedrals
        in whose doorways I have stood,
felt myself small, being taught to look upward:
two centuries in the building, sometimes more—
that is, for the ones that got finished.

Even better, I think of the ones still incomplete,
        brickwork exposed, windows of unstoried glass.

They all began with those who knew
they would never see the work
complete in their lifetime—
and this was all the more reason to begin—
and having begun, continue.

Their labour was their forgiveness
for their labour was their faith.

Of Alberta, let us make healed earth,
cleaned air, water fit for all to drink,
let the seasons return unblemished.

Let us make with the patience of cathedral builders
                    for all the world to see.

                        Earth Day, April 22, 2022.

THIS MORNING, ENERGY TRANSFORMATION IN ALBERTA AND THE INVASION OF UKRAINE

Daybreak in Alberta; gas prices rise, and
the government collects the royalties like
they'd invented fossil fuels; the party in charge
here credits itself and re-dedicates its secret war room
to an economy based on the dictum: *These are the ashes*
upon which we shall build our house.

From across the world, news of cities besieged arrives
the way news of cities besieged was the stuff of
war correspondence in the Crusades. We have learned
less than nothing, for when they made it back home,
the vanquished told their kings, *It wasn't worth it,*
and still, we talk today as if all Christendom did was win.

I am thinking about carbon capture and soil and
shutting down the coal-fired plants. I am thinking
about the tanker cars that Canadian National pulls through
Calgary every day, a pipeline in movable parts,
stealth-black, 100 tons apiece, a stupendous chain
of rolling stock, steel-ringed, oil-swelled, 700 barrels per.
How long will it take all that oil to be consumed, you ask?

The world puts 97 million barrels a day
in its bowl in the morning and has it licked clean by night.
Let's say a train has 50 tank cars on the rails:
35,000 barrels on wheels: it's used up in 30 seconds.
You should stand by the tracks and count the cars.
At 50, tell yourself: This is half a minute's worth of
fuel for the machine we have served
so faithfully and so well.

For this, people not so far from us we can't see them
in an instant are fighting for their lives—
for their homes, their streets, their apartments,
their children and parents, their art galleries and
hospitals and schools and their government and their farms.
For this, the fields of Ukraine will lie untilled
and human hunger will gnaw us all and grow.
Every day talk returns to this war
that might lead to another one, the war
that might end everything.

In October, 1962, a kindergarten teacher
gave me a form for my parents to sign,
though I only remember my mother touching it,
and crying when she gave it back,
her signature giving the school
permission to take me to a place of safety
in case of a nuclear strike. Years later
it struck me: A place of safety?

But it didn't happen. We lived.
We learned something—everyone said—
something precious
about turning away from the door
with the monster behind it our own creation.
What now,
when what seemed close a few weeks ago,
when what artists and poets and experts in climate change
gathered to make words and pictures to make a difference,
is becoming a receding future,
energy itself transformed, all our industrious doings
quickened by the sun and the wind and the
4-billion-year-old fire in the belly of the planet.
What now?

EARTH AND AIR

The manuscript for what might have been
          my second book of poems
                    could have been the last—

needy, rushed, despairing in a way
          I thought at the time was passion.

The places where I read this work
          have never invited me back.

The veteran poet I turned to for help
          told me it was words with no voice.

One trusted reader I asked for their opinion
          took it to a field, dug a hole, and threw it in.

It's there today, critiqued by the soil for decades,
perhaps unrecognizable by now.

This is the way the earth forgives.

The earth forgives us in its darkness
          where the dead and the discarded
                    are prepared like pharaohs
          for the life to come.

It forgives like the woman at the wake who
          eats the sins
                    of the guest of honour.

It forgives from under the concrete of the city
      the asphalt and the steel
           and the soles of your shoes.

The earth forgives you even though you go for days,
           or weeks, or maybe even years

                without touching.

The earth's love is a patient love,
        it will wait your whole life for you to come back.

I spread my father's ashes in a garden
        and they are now the stuff of flowers.

More often than not,
what you suffer from the earth is the suffering of your own making.

Still the earth suffers with you,
      and all the gas and dust we have raised
        cremating the earth
      still wheel above us,

longing to join the soil
        and be reborn.

AND IT BURSTS WITH LIGHT

Near the end of my travels in Ghana,
I saw a young woman begging
near the market where
I went to spend the last of my Ghanaian money,
which cannot be switched
      for other money once you leave.

I had already seen things that changed my eyes:

The generation of river-blind grandparents holding the hands
of the children bound to them by family to lead them
through the cacophonous streets.

Men with alms' bowls in their mouths, their hands fisted around
blocks of wood, hauling the legs that polio left curled like trumpet pipe
where taxi cabs from the airport sat stopped by red lights.

And then I met the woman at the market who,
said a shopkeeper, was a leper, the disease her name,
"leper", like "believer" or "follower"
essence before existence,
that essence, a terror of medieval thought.

She was looking for money. She was alone. I know.
I know.
I knew leprosy was not contagious.
I knew being within range of her breath would
put me in no danger. Still,
when I gave her the rest of my money,
I let her put her fingers on one side of the bills

while I held the other.
But after she accepted my money,
she smiled and looked me in the face,
and put out her hand again,
offering it to mine to shake,
to touch and be touched,
human being, human being,
giving me a chance to do something
my life had never asked.
I took her hand.
I thanked her. I wished her well.

When I came back from Africa, I asked Lisa to marry me.

The limits of your poetry
        are the words you never write,
                and I have never written the story of
        "the day I held a leper's hand."

Perhaps I thought that reaching
        across the kind of fearful ignorance
that knowledge alone cannot dispel
        but tells you that you must
is something I would need to do only once.

Perhaps I'd hoped that to be true,
        though I know it isn't.

Perhaps I haven't known what I would do
        if I had to do it over.

Perhaps I've never seen what I did not just
        as defying what I felt, but as in defiance of
                everything that raised me, right or wrong.
I have been less intimate with the Earth
        than those who drill for oil.

I have loved the land less
        than a rancher loves it.

The biology I studied in the 1970s
        is the biology of a planet that no longer exists.

The Earth I have known
                has always been sick.

But now the machine
we have tried to make of the world,
the pistons of its great engines,
the vaults of its boilers and
the secret labs of its chemical combinations
        and microscopic explosions are crumbling
all around us;
        the fires have leapt from their furnaces;

the Earth is a holy thing, alive, dying, terrible,
                        reaching out, and
                we cannot flee the falling plinths of the sky,
the roof of the atmosphere so shattered that
        the sun looks down with its destroyer's face.

I want to retreat into every treasured mistake I've been taught
        that got me here.

But their collapse is telling us everything we do now
must be done with love for what we have treated
                with the contempt of young thieves
            robbing their parents
and blaming them for their own dishonesty.

Here. Look here.
Here is the soil, a word that entered
our language 800 years ago
as a combination of
"tub" and "filth" to mean,
"a pig's wallowing place," it is the soil

as the miracle of microbes and elements
            below the level of our sight;
not a carbon capture machine,
        or a natural resource to be doused
with fertilizers and pesticides year after year
            until it can give no more;

the soil is a billion billion billion mouths to feed—us,
a giant mothering around the Earth
that would be dead as Mars without it;
the soil's darkness is our own. *Touch it,* says this artwork.

Touch me, says the hand I would have
shunned were it never open to me
to release error's hold, and touch—touch
the divine and giving

• • •

Richard Harrison's On Not Losing My Father's Ashes in the Flood *won international acclaim (including a full Italian translation) and a Governor General's Award for poetry in 2017. Author and editor of eight books, Richard teaches English Literature, Essay and Creative Writing at Calgary's Mount Royal University. He also leads workshops in both poetry and prose for writers across Canada.*

And it Bursts with Light, Kate Baillies.
Intaglio on handmade paper.

AND IT BURSTS WITH LIGHT
Photopolymer Image—intaglio printed with Graphic Chemical Bone Black and a mixed yellow-gold relief roll on Kitakata Natural, Chine-collé on handmade paper - cotton linters, fescue grass, clippings, poplar and aspen leaves, laserjet-printed paper strips. 2022, 45.7 x 30.4 cm.

Kate Baillies

STATEMENT

I chose the title of this mixed media print, *And It Bursts With Light*, from the climactic line in Richard Harrison's poem of the same name. This is about soil. We have walked upon it ignorant of its generous beauty. We have treated it as repugnant to the touch. We have used it without thought to the consequences. All this must change. Handmade paper speaks to our shared ideas through text and materials. Words and phrases from Richard's poem intersect with fragments of native prairie plants to form a random, pop-up dialogue with the central image. This image printed in black with a brilliant gold-yellow surface roll speaks to soil as a rich, complex ecosystem. In the form of an eyepiece view in both a micro- and tele-scope, it presents a window to a world teaming with life, glowing with the potential to learn from and care for our planet.

• • •

For over forty years, Kate Baillies' work has engaged the way in which print media creates experiences through the senses. This engagement extends to the dialogue between images and the tactile materials with which she works. Internationally recognized, Kate's work is in the collections of the Art Gallery of Nova Scotia, the Alberta Art Foundation, and the Canada Council Art Bank.

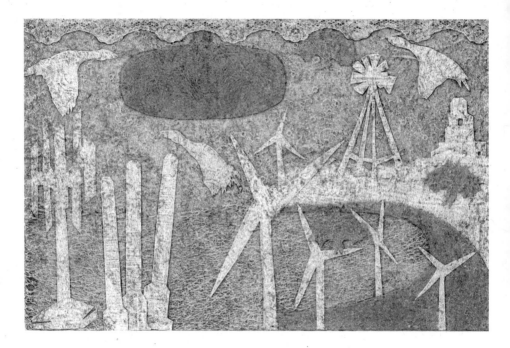

Windmills in the Rear-view Mirror,
Carole Bondaroff. Collagraph plate.
Artist's statement is at the end of this chapter.

CHAPTER TEN

THE WORLD BENEATH OUR FEET

Rosemary Griebel, Author
Carole Bondaroff, Artist

"We know more about the movement of celestial bodies
than about the soil underfoot." —*Leonardo Da Vinci*

I.

CONSIDER that the word "human" comes from the Latin word
"humus" meaning earth or ground, and Adam or Adamah in
Hebrew means earth. Being human acknowledges that we're made
from the earth, fed by the earth, and will return to the earth in some
form. As humans, we are connected and sustained by the land
throughout our life, yet we understand so little about it.

Every day we walk upon the earth and are aware of the sky over-
head and the landscape that surrounds us, but seldom think of the
furious activity only centimetres below our feet. While humans have
spent a century focused on exploring outer space and the spheres
beyond this precious Earth, there is a whole universe under our feet
that we are just starting to discover.

A vast, churning, subterranean kingdom of organisms exists in
the underworld. It is estimated that a single gram of soil may contain
as many as 4 million bacteria, 1 million fungi, 20 million filamen-
tous bacteria (actinomycetes) and 30,000 algae. Higher up the soil
food chain are the springtails and mites that prey on bacteria and

fungi. Larger still are the earthworms, ants, termites, millipedes, and beetles that fragment the organic debris, aerate the soil, and form channels for infiltration of water.

The soil beneath our feet is a living food chain, an ecological archive, and a dynamic energy force that quietly shapes the world around us. Plants, fungi, and lichens have been drawing carbon dioxide out of the air for 700 million years and putting it into the soil in an alchemical cycle of turning carbon into life. Through human intervention this complex web of life has been disrupted and contributes to climate change but could also play a significant role in reversing global warming.

II.

Growing up on a farm in east central Alberta I lived close to the land, spending unstructured days in tall grass studying those gnomic cottonwood trees and listening to the aspen trees' music, their leaves like little hands clapping in the wind. But I was also intrigued by the mysterious underground world. From an early age I had a desire to tunnel into the earth, to feel the cool dank cellar of soil around me. I had heard the popular legend that if you dig deep enough into the underground you could emerge in China. Henry David Thoreau wrote about this fanciful idea in Walden: "...There was a crazy fellow in town who undertook to dig through to China, and he got so far that, as he said, he heard the Chinese pots and kettles rattle." Yet, my desire to tunnel deep into the earth wasn't for the adventure of landing in China or any other country for that matter, but rather the comfort of being surrounded by the dark primordial world with its scent of rich, vibrant soil.

If you've ever walked through a damp forest or got down on your hands and knees to dig in the earth, you have smelled the sweet, slightly metallic scent which evokes something so deep that it is hard to describe. Scientist and author Robin Wall Kimmerer has said that the smell of soil has a physiological effect on humans, releasing oxytocin, the same chemical that promotes bonding between mother and child.

Actually, it is not the soil we smell, but a chemical released by microbes called geosmin. That scent is a clue that soil is not simply dirt, but a complex ecosystem that is alive and a wild fountain of energy. The spongy friability and sweet smell of dirt is the handiwork of trillions of microorganisms over time. It is a complex web of life that is still not yet fully understood by scientists, or those of us who work with it as gardeners or farmers. Yet it holds such hope for our future, with soil's ability to capture carbon from the atmosphere through sequestration and reduced emissions.

III.

In many ways life is a series of nested relationships. There is a concept in Hindu mythology that depicts the Earth resting on a giant turtle, which rests on another turtle, and so on. Turtles on turtles. Relationships often make little sense unless you understand their context, so let me tell you a story. It's about my family, and four generations of living on the land, but it could be about any Canadian family with a connection to conventional farming, who have undergone a paradigm shift in thinking about soil and the stewardship of the land.

Just after the turn of the twentieth century my grandfather traveled from South Dakota to Central Alberta to homestead. To receive land, the colonists had to occupy the place for a set amount of time and agree to do certain 'improvements' upon the land within a period of three years. Needless to say, there was no mention of the Indigenous Peoples who had lived on the land for thousands of years and their own relationship to the land.

To 'improve' the land, homesteaders were required to build a house, put up a fence, and 'break' the land, an apt term for plowing the soil and removing the plants living on it so crops could be sown. Homesteaders tilled and destroyed protective grasslands, although at the time they couldn't have understood the ramifications of the broken earth. It wasn't until the Dustbowl era of the 1930s, that the consequences of removing an ocean of natural grasses that held soil in place would be evident in one of North America's worst ecological disasters.

If you 'proved up' your homestead you could gain legal ownership of the land. Because there were few trees on the prairie and lumber was scarce and expensive, my grandfather's first house was a sod shack, a house made of dirt and grass, cut from slough beds. My grandmother who moved to her new sod home as a young bride from Chicago, would later recount how their sod home was permeated with soil fine as sifted flour. The persistent earth coated the table and windows and billowed up from bed and floor.

Grasslands and grazing animals have evolved together over millennia and are mutually beneficial. The land my grandfather homesteaded was shortgrass prairie, best-suited to grazing by buffalo which roamed the prairies for millennia but were driven to near-extinction in the late 1800s. Also, grasslands play a vital role in storing carbon, unlike grain fields. A prairie grass plant can have roots that can descend eight to fourteen feet below ground, and every millimeter of those roots is thrumming with microorganisms. Plowing up grasslands releases large amounts of carbon dioxide, the greenhouse gas linked to climate change, a concept that wouldn't be widely known or understood for at least another generation.

IV.

By following the government's homesteading rules my grandfather who loved the land would violate what we now know are the four soil health principles: minimization of disturbance, maximization of soil cover, increasing of biodiversity, and maximization of a living root system. But my grandfather plowed the land with a horse, trudging up and down the furrows in his hobnailed boots. In this way he knew the fields as though they were an extension of his body. The soil, plants, and insects were so close he could see and smell them, and he understood the cycles of life in the soil as it responded to the seasons but didn't fully understand the complexity of soil.

The next generation of farming would be much more apocalyptic. My father and mother farmed the land during the 50s, 60s, and 70s, which was productively abundant and ecologically disastrous with the introduction of chemicals and huge machinery that tore up the land and removed that close physical connection to the earth. My father maintained a small mixed farm, but around him large agro-industry monocultures rose up, and much of prairie wildlife, including grasslands became classified as at risk.

My brother would inherit farmland with fields that were sterile and bereft of nature due to industrial farming practices of my father's generation. It was during the next generation that my brother and sister-in-law began to shift the extractive paradigm of land ownership and food production. Their shift in awareness mirrored a larger, societal shift in the 1980s and 1990s.

My brother's journey from industrial farmer to a disciple of regenerative agriculture was the beginning of painstaking labour to restore and nourish the depleted soil on our farm. This ecological awakening greatly influenced the way my nephew now stewards the land and produces food in what is now a fourth-generation family farm. It is common sense that if you do not provide the body with nourishing food, it becomes diseased and disabled. Similarly, if you do not provide nourishment to the soil which produces the food, the soil becomes infertile and deadened. Our bodies are an extension of the earth.

V.

In simplistic terms soil is a mixture of four elements: dead and living organisms, minerals, air, and water. It's only recently that microbiologist Dr. Elaine Ingham and other soil scientists have discovered the complexity of soil and its microbial underworld of fungal material, bacteria, protozoa, and nematodes. This diverse world can descend at least seven miles below the earth's surface.

Carbon, along with the mineral matrix, are the main components of soil organic matter, and is what gives soil its structure, fertility, and ability to retain water. Through photosynthesis a plant draws carbon out of the air to form carbon compounds. What the plant doesn't need for growth it deposits through the roots to feed soil organisms.

A critical engine of the global carbon cycle are soil microbiomes, the collection of bacteria and other microbes in the soil. They are the movers and shakers of carbon sequestration. Microbes decompose the dead plant material to recycle nutrients back into the ecosystem. It is estimated that in a handful of dirt there are more individual microbes than there are humans on Earth or visible stars in the sky. It takes a village to raise a plant, as plants are dependent on these microorganisms to retain nutrients and make nitrogen available.

When the bacteria and fungi gobble up the carbon it becomes part of their bodies, and carbon keeps cycling through the food web. As the University of Alberta soil scientist, Dr. Derek MacKenzie states, there is no waste in natural ecosystems. One organism's waste is another organism's fuel. He believes as humans we need to emulate the closed energy loop of soil in all our practices including not throwing away energy that is raw kitchen scraps or wastewater.

Closed loop systems, whether in our lifestyles or agriculture can go a long way to reducing greenhouse gas emissions.

The process of decomposition is one in which soil organisms keep creating longer and longer stable carbon chains, all which contain the energy that plants create from sunlight. It is believed some pools of carbon housed in soil aggregates are so stable they can last thousands of years. In comparison, 'active' soil carbon which is found in topsoil is in continual flux between microbial hosts and the atmosphere.

VI.

In the fourth generation of family farming, my nephew and his wife, along with many other young agrarians today, have embraced a holistic approach to agriculture based on new knowledge of soil and microbiology.

This approach, called regenerative farming, is based on principles that enrich soil, increase biodiversity, improve watersheds, and enhance the ecosystem. It is nourishing rather than extractive as it actively works to capture carbon in the soil while producing more nutrient-dense food. This is an agricultural paradigm motivated by creating a healthier, more sustainable world for future generations, rather than focusing just on increased production and profit.

As basic as soil carbon is, there is still so much regenerative farmers and scientists are learning about how to maximize carbon storage. One strategy is to increase soil biology by adding beneficial microbes to stimulate the soil cycles, particularly where the land has been degraded by the use of chemicals such as herbicides, insecticides or fertilizers. For example, using compost as fertilizer adds carbon to sustain the organisms, as opposed to synthetic fertilizers which destroy the organisms in the soil.

Another strategy is to increase cover crops, perennial crops, and polycropping which increases food productivity while increasing soil health at the same time. There is also a movement to regenerate the world's grasslands as perennial grasses sequester as much or more carbon than forests, holding it in their root systems below ground so that if there is a fire no carbon is released. The Global Evergreening Alliance calls it "greening up to cool down," and together with the Savory Global Network, their goal is to capture from the atmosphere and restore to the land twenty billion tons of CO_2 annually by the year 2050.

But it's hard to manage what you can't measure. Here in Alberta, University of Alberta soil scientist Dr. Derek MacKenzie is developing a soil database app that will measure soil health and foster a better understanding of what soil management practices work best for geographic regions and the related carbon offsets. The free web-based app is being developed for farmers and other landowners to assess their soil and plot out how they can measure, maintain, and improve soil quality. The app will help maximize soil health and build knowledge among farmers of the best carbon sequestration strategies. Dr. Mackenzie believes that we are fortunate to have fine-textured soils in Alberta that have the ability to store large amounts of carbon through regenerative management. However, we need to continue to build on successful practices. As Dr. MacKenzie says, "No-till practices have already been adopted across much of the province. Now we need to recycle all of our organic waste and get it back into our soils, not landfills."

VII.

We now know that the thin skin of soil that covers much of the
planet stores vast amounts of carbon. Carbon sequestration in the
land is a complex process that is still in the early stages of understanding, and while soil sequestration alone cannot stop global
warming, the soil, trees, and plants all have a role to play in cooling
and healing our feverish planet.

The health of our soil does not require great feats of engineering.
But it does require national will to prioritize a healthy ecosystem.
The people best-poised to bring this climate solution to fruition are
the same people who steward the land and put food on our tables:
farmers and ranchers. According to Statistics Canada 2021 census,
Canada has 154 million acres of farmland, and 126 million of those
are in the Prairie provinces of Saskatchewan, Alberta, and Manitoba.

A 2017 study estimated that with better management, global
croplands have the potential to store an additional 1.85 gigatons of
carbon each year—as much as the global transportation sector emits
annually. Moreover, some scientists believe soils could continue to
sequester carbon for 20 to 40 years before they become saturated.

VIII.

The term 'plant blindness' was coined in 1999 by botanists to
bring attention to the diminishing ability of people to notice plants
and appreciate their utility to life. Ask almost anyone who has made
a road trip across the prairies what they saw of nature, and they may
talk about wildlife, but probably could not identify the many varieties
of grasses, grains, wildflowers, or trees in the landscape. It would
be even less likely that the prairie traveller would talk about seeing
alkaline soils or mud flats. The world under our feet, which is the
foundation of life, is simply invisible. And unfortunately, that which
we don't see, we tend to care less about or understand.

Soil may not have the dramatic beauty of a lush coastal rainfor-
est or an iconic glacier, but once we begin to understand soil's complexity and its role in maintaining and restoring health to the planet,
it can be seen as stunning and essential as any ecosystem on Earth.

While we search for the elusive technological bullet to deal with carbon capture, a big piece of the answer may be found under our feet. The future, as with the past, is underground in our precious earth.

Sources

Agricultural and Environmental Letters Journal (Open Source).

Can Soil Help Combat Climate Change? - State of the Planet, https://news.climate.columbia.edu/2018/02/21/can-soil-help-combat-climate-change/.

Ohio State University. CFAES Rattan Lal Center for Carbon Management and Sequestration.

Ohlson, Kristin. *The Soil Will Save Us*. Rodale Inc, 2014.

Reid, Keith. *Improving Your Soil: A Practical Guide to Soil Management for the Serious Home Gardener*. Firefly Books, 2014.

Soilfoodweb.com: Dr. Elaine Ingham's website

The USDA-NRCS website has an excellent introduction to soil biology at .

https://www.nrcs.usda.gov/wps/portal/nrcs/detailfull/national/soils/health/?cid=stelprdb1048783

My thanks to University of Alberta professor and soil scientist, Dr. Derek MacKenzie, for reviewing this article and providing helpful comments.

ODE TO SOIL

Rosemary Griebel

"Even the broken letters of the heart spell earth."
~ Daniel Thompson

O sacred ground, O dark world,
O teeming engine of life. I bury my face
in your musky cellar, sweet geosmin,
scent of microbes' handiwork,
intimate taste of vegetal storm and thunder.

O gratitude for plants and trees
for they eat light and carbon, root pull
of spangled banquet to the underworld.
O praise the somber work of earth's humble
labourers: invisible algae, fungi, and bacteria.
Praise the springtails, beetles, and worms
who devour debris, aerate our feverish earth,
stitch carbon into fungal networks.

O sacred ground, you hold the breath and bone
of ancestors. Yet we have degraded you to filth
broken your masterpiece with tillage and tilth.
We force you to belch up carbon, regurgitate
chemicals in which you're doused, bleaching
the land, poisoning food and waterways.

O generosity of earth. Every step on the ground
borne on the backs of millions of invertebrates.
Help us appreciate your incalculable mysteries,
and the alchemy with which you transform
death into life. Our existence, our future
is rooted in your munificent dark body.

. . .

*Rosemary Griebel is a Calgary writer and professional
librarian, with a passion for community building, nature,
and story. Growing up on the prairies she developed a deep
respect for the language of the land and its inhabitants.
In addition to her collection of poetry,* Yes, *her award-
winning poetry has appeared in* The Best Canadian Poetry
in English, *as well as on CBC Radio, literary magazines,
anthologies, and chapbooks. In 2019 one of her poems
was chosen for Alberta's first literary landmark, as part of
Project Bookmark Canada's CanLit Trail.*

Celestial Crisis, Carole Bondaroff.
Etching and Chine-collé.

WINDMILLS IN THE REAR-VIEW MIRROR
Collagraph plate, 2022, 33 x 48.3 cm

CELESTIAL CRISIS
Etching and Chine-collé, 2022, 48.3 x 33 cm.

Carole Bondaroff

STATEMENT

Windmills in the Rear-view Mirror evolved while driving through a field of modern electricity-generating wind turbines. I was struck by thoughts of how things have changed. The rear-view mirror suggests a window into the past and I fused the contemporary agricultural challenges with those of the early farming pioneers.

Celestial Crisis features my interpretation of Japanese artist Hokusai's woodblock print entitled 'The Great Wave off Kanagawa' with Mount Fuji in the background. The famed 'Three Sisters' of the Canadian Rockies, are subtly indicated in the clouds, connecting the east to the west. Portrayed is a giant rogue wave which represents the energy of the oceans. Additional elements include three smaller plates, with 'chine-collé appliqué' (Japanese washi paper,) depicting lunar phases which govern the tides: Harnessing Tidal Power—Energy of the Future?

• • •

Carole Bondaroff, an active artist and art educator, lives in Calgary at the Heart Studio; an exhibition and teaching facility that has mentored thousands of aspiring artists. She is a long-time member of the Alberta Society of Artists, and a founding member of the Alberta Printmakers' Society. Her work has been collected internationally by the Canada Council Art Bank, the Alberta Foundation for the Arts, the Consulate of Japan, and the Royal Palace in Monaco.

Through Tempered, Rose-Coloured Glasses, Heather Urness.
Woodcut on five layers of translucent synthetic paper.
Artist's statement is at the end of this chapter.

CHAPTER ELEVEN

PLANNING FOR THE FUTURE AS OUR WORLD BURNS AND WE MOVE TO THE SUBURBS/ IN TRANSITION

Kathryn Gwun-Yeen 君妍 Lennon, Author
Heather Urness, Artist

I'M RAISED TO TURN OFF THE LIGHTS when I leave a room, to run off the tap mid-way through brushing my teeth so as not to waste water. The ozone hole is a real threat. The Montreal Protocol is signed in 1987. The Kyoto Protocol in 1997. In 2006, I am in my first year of university, majoring in environmental studies, when the Stern Review on the Economics of Climate Change is released. The boomers (our professors) tell us: It will be up to you, the youth to fix this mess we're in. Good luck. But my friends already rarely eat meat, drink out of mason jars, campaign for fair trade coffee, guerrilla garden, and dumpster dive. They teach me, "if it's yellow, let it mellow, if it's brown, flush it down." But when I go home to visit, my mom tells me it's nice to have me back home, but it would be nice if I could remember to flush the toilet. The youth, we are the future, they say. A few years later, I return to Edmonton. "There must be lots of environmental work there," people say. Not really. It's 2010, and riding a bike to work here is seen as a death-defying, banner-waving, environmental statement. People assume that because I do that I must also be vegetarian. When Greta Thunberg launches Skolstrejk, my now

30-something-year-old peers join the chorus, saying, the youth are the future. The youth are the future. But the youth are also anxious with climate grief. The boomers—they ask why we despair so much? Why are we so gloomy?

And now, planning for the future as our world burns and we move to the suburbs, takes starting from a deep, dark place, and learning to greet paralyzing grief with gentleness. And in this process, I always come back to food. Contemplating the brokenness of local, regional and global food systems can be paralyzing—the depletion of soil nutrients, the impacts of climate change on agriculture, the loss of biodiversity and traditional knowledge, dependence on food that has to travel great distances and is grown by workers with little protections, the struggle for farmers to earn fair prices. But for me, food is also from where I draw hope and strength. And the acts of reclaiming knowledge, building soil health, fostering intergenerational connections, restoring relationships to land and water and place and each other. And on the darkest days, I always come back to: what meal can I craft from what I have to work with? What can I plant in my garden?

In reflection on the layers in a garden ecosystem, the following poem moves through a garden's seasons, drawing inspiration from the traditional Chinese lunar-solar calendar. This traditional calendar is known as the Agricultural Calendar or *Nongli*, as the calendar divides the year into seasons for agriculture, which is the principal economy of the country. The Agricultural Calendar is an integrated lunar-solar calendar *(Yinyangli)* as it embraces the movement of the moon as well as that of the Sun. I see parallels between translocating traditional agricultural knowledge to my home in Alberta, and translating traditional agricultural knowledge as the world shifts around us and seasons change—in relation to energy futures, this ancient agricultural knowledge needs to be adapted.

They say that there is privilege in thinking of climate change as an apocalypse, because so many in this world have already endured, survived, resisted the ends of their worlds through colonization, displacement, genocide, famine, war, migration, gentrification, solastalgia. Those who have survived and continue to endure colonization, famine, war, migration, poverty and grief. I remember to breathe in, draw strength from the strength of the tenacious of the earth. This is not to say there will be a happy ending. But as my artist partner, Heather, reminded me, do we live for the ending or live for the living? The process of reflecting on this project has brought me to an in-between space: a mid-ground. And somewhere between the world is ending, and everything will be okay, there is living.

• • •

立春 Lì Chūn
Start of Spring Month

You come out into the world smoothly and nonchalantly
the same way you come into our awareness:
an unexpected home birth in the early
hours of a frigid February day.
We grew you last summer on food from our garden:
peas, spinach, kale, chard, beans, corn, tomatoes, potatoes.
Cherries from the backyard, berries from u-picks.
Black chernozemic soils around our city.
We are learning all the names of things
our mothers call babies in their mother tongues:
baby shrimp, baby duck, baby bear, baby cat.
I wonder who you will be, who you will love, who will love you.
I wonder what your relationship will be to this land.
I wonder what world you will live in, what seasons you will live with,
how you will move through it all as it all falls apart.
I hope we can fill you with enough love to
float your life raft through it all.

清明 Qīng Míng
Clear and Bright Moon Month

Stop reading the news, turn off your phone. Get out of bed.
Breathe in and out, and in and out.
Pull on some jeans, some boots, socks optional. At least for this
morning, while the light is honey and blue, set down your grief,
leave it on the kitchen table in the dish where you keep spare
change. Pull out those seeds that your ancestors carried in their
pockets as they fled war, fled famine. Open the door, set one foot in
front of the other. Step out onto cracked concrete and the muck
and grit and skeletons of last year's leaves. Greet the hare with one
eye. Greet the irises pushing up so green it hurts. Pick a piece of
earth, small enough to love. A terracotta pot, an old milk carton,
a strip of land, a raised bed. Make a plan or follow your instincts.
Pull your fingers through the soil. Scatter seeds. Add water. This is
enough for today.

惊蛰 Jīng Zhé
Awakening of Insects Month

What a time to bring a baby into the world, settle down, grow up. In
the next few decades, the world will continue to get darker, hotter,
harder, scarier, more dangerous, more unpredictable. What can we
do? Not much? But I draw strength from thinking that all of us here
today are descended from a parent, a grandparent, a great-grand-
parent, and so on, who survived war or famine or exile or depres-
sion—whether by good luck, or wit, or strength of spirit.

谷雨 Gǔ Yǔ
Grain Rain Month

I drop a Pyrex container and it shatters into a billion smithereens and dust. I'm not able to stop you, my son, though I watch it in slow motion. What have we done? What hardships, inequities, injustices continue to be perpetuated in the face of the climate crisis? What world have you arrived into? How will we prepare you to live through the challenges ahead? How much can our little actions change anything when our political leaders continue to prop up oil and gas and prioritize immediate (perceived) gains over all else? What can we do?

大暑 Dà Shǔ
Major Heat Month

We purchase a mid-century house in a car-oriented neighborhood in a land-locked prairie city.
It is hot, poorly insulated, without air conditioning. We shelter in the basement. We look into how to qualify for federal and municipal energy retrofit rebates. The Energy Retrofit Accelerator Program and Greener Homes Grants programs are barely decipherable or accessible to us, middle-class, new home-owners. How will these types of policies make the urgent change we need, especially when energy poverty is a hurdle to many to just pay minimum energy bills, let alone upgrade their homes?

Retrofit. To install new parts in something constructed in another time. To adapt to a new purpose or need. To work from home in a home designed for a time when stay-at-home wives waved their husbands off to work. Homes that leak energy and waste water. The lifeless lawns. Our to-do list: improve attic insulation, install solar, convert lawn to xeriscape, plant native plants and a vegetable garden. A week before our first big project, the City cancels the retrofit program due to over-subscription.

处暑 Chù Shǔ
Limit of Heat Month

We harvest three, shriveled cherry tomatoes from our community
garden plot. We were absentee landlords in this year's heat. I am a
hypocrite. After years of working on community food security, and
three years on my neighbourhood's community garden wait list,
I'm the gardener that gardeners love to hate. The one who lets their
weeds grow tall and abandons their plot at the height of the harvest.

白露 Bái Lù
White Dew Month

We learn that the linear off-leash dog park bordering our home is
the pathway of the TransMountain petroleum pipeline. In operation
since 1953, the pipeline predates the 1960s construction date of our
home. Welcome to Petrolia. What can you do? Pipeline corridors
underpin many of the green spaces in this city. Three-hundred-
thousand barrels of petroleum products run by my house each day,
as they set out on their 1,150 km. journey to the coast. A friend dryly
texts, "It will be so easy for you to set up a blockade." Another jokes
that I'll be able to hoist protest signs without leaving my property.
Sunbather, or pipeline protester?

A park without a name, I call it Pipeline Park. It's important to name
the things we want to change. With a clear view, we get neon pink
and purple sunrises to the south, and sky-splitting sunsets to the
north. And all the puppies and bikes our kid desires.

秋分 Qiū Fēn
Autumnal Equinox

We take our little one to the forest, to the ocean, to the river.
The world around him sparkles into focus as he discovers the
power of naming things:
Puppy. Garden. Cheese. Flower. Birch. Moon. Stars.

• • •

Kathryn Gwun-Yeen 君妍 Lennon is the co-creator of Hungry Zine, a food-focused publication. She has worked in and around food policy and food security for over a decade. She sees the acts of growing, cooking, and sharing food as ways of honouring those who have come before, imagining just and sustainable futures, and cultivating relationships to people and place. Her work has been published in Living Hyphen, Ricepaper Magazine, the Ethnic Aisle, Spacing Magazine, *and* Alternatives Journal.

Through Tempered, Rose-Coloured Glasses, Heather Urness.
Process images: carving the linoleum and cutting the prints
from the translucent paper. Detail of constructed print.

THROUGH TEMPERED, ROSE-COLOURED GLASSES
Five-layered woodcut relief printed on translucent recyclable synthetic and pulp-based papers with water-soluble ink and paint. Varied edition of 27, 2022, 48.3 x 33 cm.

Heather Urness

STATEMENT

I am, by nature, hopeful | Hopeful but not naive
I know there is no simple answer to the climate crisis
It is a layered hot mess | The magnitude of it feels overwhelming
I take comfort knowing many are seeking solutions
Finding answers in non-advertised spaces
Creating possibilities in unexpected places | they are looking for
Connections | Both literal and figurative
Some new and some old | Exploring the link between science and art—
to point the way | they are looking at
Communities | Think: Soil. Mycelium. Fungus. Food. Native grasslands.
Plants. People. The air these communities breathe. The water they drink
| seekers consider the
Ripple Effect Plants draw down carbon. Soil sequesters carbon.
Honeycombs of graphene offer pockets of nutrition and hope
It is a cycle of growth and repair—not despair. A cycle of the sun/flower
and the moon and the seasons | they explore
Regeneration (create again) | Plants for renewable, bright green
energy | Fungus for building blocks and for changing the conversation
Biodiversity for vast threads of connection ... community wide | hopeful

• • •

Mohkinstsis (Calgary) based multi-media print artist Heather Urness has been in the business of creating images for decades. With a background in graphic design and a BFA in printmaking and drawing, Heather likes to play fast and loose with traditional printmaking techniques while embracing new, greener methods. Her work explores the connection between the familiar and the unexpected.

We Can Create a Future for Alberta in Which No Person is Left Behind,
Hannah Gelderman. Silkscreen.
Artist's statement is at the end of this chapter.

CHAPTER TWELVE

ENERGY POVERTY

Alexis Kienlen, Author
Hannah Gelderman, Artist

Empower Me

Amy is a single mother who owns her own home, which she shares
with her twelve-year-old son, Will. They live in north Edmonton, in
an older two-storey. Amy struggles with the bills, especially when
it comes to heating her home. Her furnace is old, and she suspects
her house could be better insulated. There are drafts around the
windows, particularly in Will's room. To keep it warm in the winter, Amy puts a heater in his bedroom. Amy is constantly anxious
about being cold and getting sick. If she gets sick, she might have to
miss work. Sometimes Amy wants to buy extra food at the grocery
store, but she goes without because she knows she needs to pay her
mortgage and her energy bill first. One time, she had her power
turned off in the summer. At another point, she had a limiter put
on her electricity, which meant she and Will had to cook in the dark.
She is not sure what all the problems are with her home, but she is
aware there are problems. However, she doesn't have the money to
fix them.

Amy and Will are fictional people, but they represent the one
in four Albertans who live in energy poverty. When people are
in energy poverty, they spend a disproportionate amount of their

137

income on energy costs. Because Amy's home is older and needs work, it is not energy efficient. Her energy costs are about six times the Canadian average. In Alberta, about 18 percent of Albertans, (just under 240,000 homes) spend more than double the national average of their income on energy. In Canada, 2.8 million people are living in energy poverty. Single parents (80 percent of whom are women), seniors, immigrants, newcomers, and Indigenous Peoples are more likely to have challenges paying for their energy bills and are more likely to be living in energy poverty. People in Canada can also be energy poor if they are spending more than 30 percent of their income on energy bills. The cost to heat homes and the kind of energy used varies from province to province, so it is difficult to get an accurate image of spending across the country.

But energy poverty is not a problem just in Canada. It's a global· problem that prevents people from adapting to climate change and moving to net zero carbon emissions. People living in energy poverty can't meet their own energy needs, and this prevents them from embracing more efficient technologies. These people are unable to make a just transition to cleaner energy. People have been aware of energy poverty since the 1990s, and in most provinces in Canada, there are government programs that can help people get things like new heat pumps, furnaces, windows, and insulation.

Empower Me is a non-profit group working to help people in energy poverty. Yasmin Abraham, the vice president, and co-founder of Empower Me, said energy poverty makes it hard for people to make decisions about paying their rent or mortgage or paying for food or other household needs. "Because of the intersection of energy costs and housing structure, this is not just a poverty issue or an income issue," she said. Energy poverty can have mental, physical, and multi-generational impacts. People may be living in conditions that are too warm or too cold. They may experience the stress of paying late bills, threats of eviction, mental health impacts, hypothermia or overheating, and problems with cardio, pulmonary or respiratory disease.

If Amy and Will were clients of Empower Me, the organization would help them reduce their energy consumption. They would make upgrades to their windows, and insulation, and purchase a better furnace for the home. These changes would improve Amy and Will's energy efficiency and reduce greenhouse gases. Will wouldn't need to use a heater in his bedroom anymore. Amy now has more money to buy food at the grocery store. She is sick less and doesn't have to worry about missing work. Her overall income is more stable.

In 2018, Empower Me launched its first energy poverty program in Calgary and helped low-income households in Calgary reduce their energy consumption. The challenge now, in Alberta, is to create a sustained program that can make a real change for households and help lift them out of energy poverty.

Urban planning and energy poverty

Development in cities can impact housing affordability and people's ability to pay for their energy use. "When we think of urban planning, it's how we use our land and land development," said Stefanie Drozda, an Edmonton-based program specialist with the Climate Innovation Fund, operated by the Alberta Ecotrust Foundation. In the past, planners have occasionally looked at different land uses, separating commercial or industrial from residential land use. People who are in energy poverty need to be considered in urban planning. "In cities where it isn't easy to access energy infrastructure; that can be a contributor to energy poverty," she said. Developing a diversity of housing options and variability in density of urban spaces can make housing more affordable. Existing houses may need to be upgraded over time to be energy efficient.

"Green spaces and infrastructure can impact peoples' experience with energy poverty," said Drozda. "Maybe less so in Alberta, but even as our climate changes in Alberta, and we have higher temperatures and more extreme weather, things like green infrastructure can impact the temperature of our neighbourhoods." High temperatures can create the phenomenon of urban heat islands, where spaces built primarily of concrete, with few trees and green infrastructure, increase the ambient heat to even-higher temperatures. This places more stress on the energy costs of nearby residents, who must pay more to cool their homes.

Drozda said that equity needs to be considered when planning the actions and policies of municipalities and governments, and their effects on residents. "When we are thinking about putting in programs and policies that are equity-centred, we have to think about them being intersectional in nature, and it's about removing systemic barriers," she said.

Policies and programs need to be co-created with developers in the community, with solutions addressing root causes, and gathering data to address all inequalities. Cities, municipalities, and governments may want to invest in programs that offer training for energy transition jobs and reduce barriers for those who may be systemically underemployed or underrepresented to ensure everyone can benefit from the energy transition.

Transportation and energy poverty are related. "When you're looking at how we could increase the density of our city (including multifamily homes, apartments, townhouses, and duplexes), we must think about how people move around. So, if people can access services close to their neighbourhood; that can result in low-cost or easily accessible means of transportation, like biking or walking," she said. The more we can shift modes of transportation to walking and biking, the more that reduces the need to burn fossil fuels and it improves air quality. Electric vehicles are considered zero-emissions, but in Alberta, natural gas is used to produce electricity. This means that electrical vehicles still produce some emissions, but they are more efficient than internal combustion engines, thereby producing fewer greenhouse gases and having zero tailpipe emissions.

Buildings account for about 40 to 60 percent of emissions in Calgary and Edmonton. "They provide a really big opportunity to reduce emissions," said Drozda. "When we look at energy efficiency programs, the ones that exist in Canada are focused on rebates. You have to pay for an upgrade to put in new windows, with insulation. You have to have the means to pay and then get refunded with the rebate after," she said. This creates a barrier for many low-income people.

Another option is the Clean Energy Improvement Program, which is a financing program. It provides low-interest loans that can be paid back through taxes. "You have to have the means to take on more debt or have the money to pay for it upfront. When we're looking at our programming that influences energy efficiency, we have to take into account that the programs are not for everyone. Folks who are of low or moderate income don't have the means to pay for upgrades. Really, the best way to address this is to have support that targets those who are most in need and who may be hard to reach. So, if we have cultural or linguistic barriers to accessing services, the solution to that is a no-cost turnkey upgrade. You want to increase affordability, and in the long term, that will help lower the risk and impact rising energy costs. By improving these households, people also have safer homes that are more comfortable and safer to live in as well." Alberta is the only province or territory in Canada without a program for energy poverty. Drozda said creating such a program is the number one goal for Alberta Ecotrust and those working in the energy poverty sector in this province.

SAVE THE EARTH, STAY IN BED

Alexis Kienlen

don't go to work or shower,
just stay in bed.

no need to buy clothes,
stay in bed.

go to bed earlier,
sleep in later,
turn the lights off,
conserve energy.

stay in bed alone,
read a book,
turn your phone off,
read by your window light,
or light a candle.

stay in bed with a friend,
make a pillow fort,
you don't have to go out for coffee,
if you want to share secrets.

stay in bed with your dog,
stay in bed with your cat,
no need for extra blankets.
stay in bed with your lover,
make your own entertainment.

power everything down,
just stay in bed.

• • •

Alexis Kienlen is a writer of Chinese and Caucasian descent who lives in Treaty 6 (Edmonton). She holds an International Studies degree from the University of Saskatchewan, a Graduate Diploma in Journalism from Concordia University, and a Food Security Certificate from Toronto Metropolitan University. She currently works as an agricultural journalist for the Alberta Farmer *newspaper. Alexis has written two books of poetry,* She Dreams in Red *and* 13, *a biography about a Sikh civil rights activist, and a novel called* Mad Cow. *She reads a lot, cooks, and loves going for walks and playing classical guitar.*

Process images by Hannah Gelderman. Carving and printing
linocuts; screen printing the digitized linocut prints.

WE CAN CREATE A FUTURE
Silkscreen, 2022, 43.2 x 27.9 cm.

Hannah Gelderman

STATEMENT

"We can create a future for Alberta in which no person is left behind" is the closing phrase in the article In "Lieu of Lightbulbs: A Look at Energy Poverty in Alberta" by Yasmin Abraham and Emma Gammans. Writer Alexis Kienlen and I drew from this article as we collaborated for the Energy Futures Portfolio and focused on the topic of Energy Poverty. Alexis's writing is specific and very informative and my artwork complements her piece by offering a bigger picture vision for Alberta. Energy justice is a necessary part of systemic change, as we work to build a province that offers justice, clean energy, good work, and dignity for all who live here. I created all of the imagery for this print by carving linoleum blocks, which I then hand printed and scanned. I digitally arranged the imagery, exposed the digital printout to a silkscreen, and produced the final edition as silkscreen prints.

• • •

Hannah Gelderman (she/her) is a visual artist, an arts educator and a climate justice organizer, living in Amiskwaciwâskahikan (Edmonton, Alberta). In 2020 she graduated with a Master of Education in Leadership Studies from the University of Victoria where she focused her research on art and climate justice. She continues to be most energized by projects that exist at the intersection of visual arts and climate.

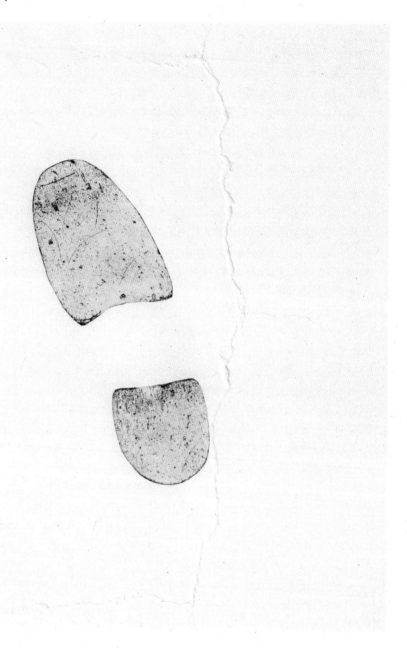

a false exodus, Katie Bruce.
Etching, Chine-collé and embossing on rag paper.
Artist's statement is at the end of this chapter.

CHAPTER THIRTEEN

THE IN-BETWEEN PEOPLE

Emma Gammans, Author
Katie Bruce, Artist

THEY TRUDGE THROUGH SNOW into the belly of a dwindling forest. It's different than they remember, bleaker. The trees—white spruce, tamarack, poplar—are devoid of branches, a colony of windswept trunks left to wither. In the wake of assault, the boreal forest has grown vulnerable, displaced and uprooted like the people; its trees shiver as the cold envelops the country. Years ago, people spoke only of the heat. Of the floods and the wildfires that sent smoke creeping into the cities. Amid the smog, a heavy sun smouldered like the hot tip of a branding iron. Perhaps it was because the summer months were so astonishing, so glaringly different than they had been decades before, that no one thought much of the cold. They never spoke of it. Even now, they do not speak of it. They only feel it.

Carried by a gentle gait, rhythmic and sure-footed, Jacob pushes forth, his boots sinking into the snow. Ellie follows in his tracks, a trail of cratered prints forming behind them. As they walk, she thinks of home, the way it used to be; for a moment the forest begins to shrink. Memory creeps into her extremities, dipping her body in the fleeting warmth of imagined fires produced with the flick of a switch. Unplanned and effortless, they were not true fires, only illusion. Still, she'd welcomed the warmth and the sudden eruption of light. Now, imploring tranquility in the midst of this trembling forest, she yearns for her painless past.

The transition, people said, would be transitory, a period marked by acute growing pains. At first, Ellie believed it would be temporary, that she would somehow find her way into a new world, but after shivering and sweating her way through the past five years, she has come to endure the distortion of time; she feels the way it can stretch or freeze altogether. Between the cost of energy and her dwindling income, she has lived half a decade in a home she can barely afford to heat or cool. And she is not alone. Pain is a sign of evolution, said the prime minister in a briefing last week. There is no need to panic, he said. Help is on the way. It may be true, but subsidies have dwindled in the last few years while electricity bills have quadrupled and the cost of food has yet to crest. Ellie knows she should have seen it coming. There were certainly enough signs. But she, like most Albertans, chose to ignore them. On occasion, there were outliers, people like Jacob who'd predicted the downfall. Welcomed it, even. It was as though he'd been waiting all his life to embrace this quiet, frigid landscape.

Pausing, he pivots, turning to look Ellie in the eyes.

—I see the end of the clearing, he says, pushing through the last of the forest's barren trees.

The phase-out of natural gas had been a convoluted process. Rural electrification in Alberta came last, just as it had in the 1900s. Cities like Calgary and Edmonton transitioned first, paving the way towards a low-carbon future, bending the cost curve. But the price of electricity still soared, leaving people to scramble for alternatives. They waded into the woods, harkening back to a pre-industrial era, to the historic heating methods of the nineteenth century. At first, people came from the cities and the neighbouring towns, bearing sharp axes and chainsaws. It didn't take long for the felling of trees to become outlawed. Relying on wood to heat homes, the government declared, was beginning to threaten vital ecosystems and was actively hampering emission reduction efforts. These announcements always seemed to draw on the language of science to separate a reality steeped in research from that which was born of lived experience.

—I see it, says Ellie, trying to sound optimistic. She can't bring herself to complain around Jacob since he always seems happiest in the woods, as if there is something profoundly instinctual about wandering the forest. Swaying, he plods ahead sporting an oversized backpack, the kind people used to take on long trips abroad. Backpacking, people called it at a time when they could still choose suffering, as though it were a badge of honour, a way of fortifying oneself against the many temptations produced by wealth.

Pushing beyond the clearing, the pair disappears under a thick, drooping canopy. Jacob tosses his bag aside and unpacks a rusting buck saw. He clambers up the nearest tree, then begins to toss branches into the snow. A small loophole, since the felling of trees involves targeting the trunks. New regulations made no mention of boughs.

For now, at least. Weighed down by bitterness, Ellie gathers them slowly, their bark peeling into tight curlicues. She wonders how time turned in on itself, how it learned to move backwards. This, as the world's politicians, engineers, and economists built the future around themselves, as if any number of tidy solutions could have made the world right. It was always about the numbers and never about the people. The news outlets were just as committed to a cold and distant form of numeral reporting wherein they spoke of the "1.3 million Canadians living in darkness." Yet they'd never know the people whose stories they were failing to tell, the children doing their homework by torchlight, or the women whose hands have grown dry and cracked from washing clothes in cold water using stone and a bar of soap. These are the In-Between people, those caught between worlds. The poverty divide in Canada has never been so vast and the In-Between people belong on neither side; they never benefited from the transition in the way that many other, more privileged Canadians did. At the same time, they have a roof over their heads, their situations far less dire than the thousands of refugees living off food stamps.

Their stories, it seems, belong only in the shadows of the forest.

Once they've filled Jacob's backpack with kindling and a bundle of thick branches, he and Ellie begin the trek home. It feels just as long as the walk in, if not longer and Ellie listens to the sound of snow crunching beneath her boots in militaristic cadence.

—I know everything's harder now, but it feels good to have a mission, doesn't it?

—Depends on your definition of good, says Ellie. She speaks teasingly to avoid deflating his energy.

—Like we earned something, you know? Didn't just receive another handout.

—We never received handouts, she says. We worked, life was still hard before, it was just... different. I think you're forgetting.

—I guess I just feel like humans were meant to live this way, Jacob continues. Like, I don't know, somehow life got too easy or something. Like we started making problems out of nothing.

—That's a little simplistic, Ellie argues, easy isn't always bad.

—Well look at Scott, he says. He's sort of a miserable fuck, don't you think?

—I don't, actually. Besides, I can't say I'd turn down his life if the opportunity presented itself.

Jacob shrugs, growing silent. Ellie thinks of Scott's many reasons to be happy. Her brother has everything he had before: an immaculate home, a massive greenhouse filled with cherry tomatoes and grapevines, even a heated garage. She thinks of the electric fireplace in his living room, the way tomorrow—Christmas Eve— she'll be in his home and feel warm again. She'll find herself caught in a trance, watching the fire dance as though real.

The forest glistens, a sunlit chamber echoing with the songs of chickadees and the sound of a garrulous wind. When they finally emerge from the clearing, they find Jacob's snowmobile parked by a dilapidated fence and an old sign, spray painted red.

No trespassing, it used to say until someone painted over it, making it illegible. The entire community has embraced this rationale: no one is breaking the rules if they don't know the rules to begin with. There was a time when Ellie might have scoffed at this logic, but nowadays it's sound enough. It has to be.

—Hop on, says Jacob after securing his backpack to a skimmer behind the Ski-Doo. No one drives much anymore; there aren't enough used EVs on the market yet and even with subsidies for new vehicles, one still needs the cash upfront. On the other hand, with the last of Alberta's unregulated extraction caught and turned belly up, there's never enough supply of gasoline on the black market.

Ellie clambers onto the second seat and wraps her arms around Jacob's torso. They've been friends since childhood but somehow in the absence of so many things, she's started to see him differently. He's stronger now. In a strange way, he seems like more of a man. Someone she might desire.

He revs the engine and they gather speed, gliding past forsaken houses with plastic-covered windows, old newspapers clinging to unwashed glass. The town is quiet, progressively insignificant. Unshovelled sidewalks merge from the edge of town towards one central boulevard. Once the beating heart of this small community, it is now a deserted remnant of a government that spent its time focused on a just transition but who, in a hurry, left half its people eclipsed. The oilfield workers upskilled and reskilled, leveraged their expertise to power the green transition. Ex-rig workers gained employment as wind techs, and solar installers, learned to scale 100-metre wind turbines in the provincial south. They may have taken a $100k pay cut but they're employed all the same, at least for now. There aren't enough maintenance jobs, and installations have already begun to slow. Still, they'd taken their chances and left town, leaving businesses to shutter. The community dried up. Ellie herself endeavours to leave but there's always something holding her back, the rental cost of a one-bedroom apartment in Edmonton, for instance, sometimes seems doable, at least until a landlord asks for rent plus a one month's security deposit.

As they motor up the hill towards a small two-bedroom bunga-low, Ellie clings to Jacob's body. It's the same house in which Ellie grew up—a house she inherited too soon. The yellow is already fading and the stucco cracked. During the summer months, its atrophied exterior is obscured by sunflowers and the rose bush her mother planted years ago, but in the winter it speaks only of decay. Now it is just her and Jacob, an anomalously empty house in a community where most families have banded together, where every second or third house is boarded up and abandoned.

They make it home at dusk and park the snowmobile in an empty garage where Jacob secures it to a d-hook using a set of thick cables. The sun, a bright pink streak on the horizon, signals the last of the day's crepuscular light. Grabbing the backpack, Jacob stomps up a set wooden stairs leading to the back door; they creak under the weight of his body. Ice sloughs off the railing, gouging the snow as it falls. Ellie follows, peering over the neighbour's fence on her way in. She spots the elderly couple next door cooking dinner on a small stove as laundry dries on a nearby rack. Inside, she and Jacob keep their hats on. Though warmer, the walls are still cold to the touch. The windows are icy and florescent; frost, a blooming gar-den in the middle of winter.

Jacob unpacks the bundle of sticks and kindling, placing the wood on a blue tarp near the fireplace. He cracks his fingers before scooping a pile of ash from the hearth, disposing of it in a metal bucket.

—You going to show me how it's done? he asks.

Ellie nears the fireplace, kneeling beside him, her knees digging into the splintered hardwood. He looks at her gently and time fades for a brief moment. She gathers a few pieces of kindling and some dry moss stockpiled from the summer. Once she has built a small tipi, he hands her a lighter. Targeting a tuft of moss, she observes as it bursts into a full-bodied flame, then she places her cheek near the ground, exhales. The fire grows smaller, then quickly doubles in size, its flames swaying, elongating as if to search for the stars. Jacob hands her a few larger branches and they arrange them into a second tipi, watching as the fire travels upward, illuminating the living room. A light brown rug, stained with ash, extends across the floor. A corduroy couch sags under an old patchwork quilt. The familiarity of home cannot be underestimated, no matter how tired-looking it's become.

When the fire eventually steadies, the pair scootch nearer, warming the tips of their fingers, welcoming the heat as it melts into their skin. Jacob retrieves the quilt from the couch and wraps it around their shoulders, pulling Ellie closer.

—Nothing quite like it, he says, looking at the fire, then at Ellie.

—Perhaps, she says, closing her eyes.

—So are you sure you want to go tomorrow? Jacob asks.

—It's Christmas, it makes sense to be with family.

—Well aren't we? At least kind of?

—I suppose. You could always come, you know, to Scott's.

—Nah, Jacob sighs, you know we don't get on.

—You could try... Besides, it'll be nice to have a change of pace.

—I'm good, he says. I like where we are, but I'll drop you at the bus in the morning.

Swaddled in the old quilt, they fall asleep together, lulled by the sound of crackling flames. Ellie dreams of the woods, only this time she is moving backwards and the trees are lush and complete.

In the morning, Jacob drops Ellie at a bus stop near the edge of town where she waits at the side of a glistening highway, light glinting as ice clings to the asphalt. In the ditch, there is a bright orange sign featuring the image of a bus and the words Route 32. She watches the road, shivering. The bus should arrive any minute, though sometimes they're late due to bad weather.

She waits until the last minute to trigger a solar-powered safety light, allowing the bus to spot her and slow to a crawl. Even with their low power draw, the lights aren't always reliable. Between storms and sporadic grey skies, the batteries occasionally lack charge at which point one can only hope the driver will stop.

Ellie finds her seat at the back of a busy bus. They are always crowded during the holidays as people travel between cities to visit family. She peers out the window as the coach regains speed. With better long-distance transit, the roads are less busy than they used to be. To her side, the fields stretch on, endlessly white save an occasional barn or grain silo. An owl, perched on a fence, takes flight as the bus rattles by. Ellie watches it soar freely; eventually it fades into the distance like everything else.

When she arrives at the terminal, she finds Marla waiting in the parking lot. Her sister-in-law has never been particularly conversational, but when asked about the ride Ellie tells her she slept most of the way. Marla nods.

—Where's your bag? she asks, peering at the small purse strung across Ellie's chest.

—I've got a toothbrush and pyjamas, says Ellie, patting the bag.

Exiting the terminal, they take a long ramp out to a busy thoroughfare before merging onto a two-lane highway. At once, the city sprawls and climbs upward. Despite new communities cropping up at the edge of every quadrant, unprecedented levels of migration continue to fuel an ongoing housing crisis. Newly built high-rises congest the downtown, gathering in tight, glassy clusters. Ellie knows the city has its own challenges but she still feels a slight sting when she considers her own worthless house stuck in a market-less ghost town. Moving would entail starting over. Then again, she supposes, the refugees fleeing flooded coastal regions started from scratch too.

After some time, they pass an ice-covered reservoir then turn right into a gated neighbourhood lined with aspen trees and long, well-kept driveways. Ellie spots Scott and Marla's house at the end of a cul-de-sac.

—Scott should be home soon, says Marla, pulling the vehicle into the garage. She plugs it in before inviting Ellie inside.

Marla flits about the kitchen, restlessly. She opens the oven to check on dinner, a roast turkey, before wiping down the cupboards with a soapy cloth for the third time. She never stops moving as Ellie sits at the island, watching. The countertop is made of marble, *bianco lasa,* says Marla. Sustainably mined. It's soft and white, subdued like an ocean fog with dark grey veins crashing into each other.

—Can I do anything? Ellie asks. Marla simply says, no.

—You sure? I don't mind.

—I'm sure.

She looks upon Ellie with pity and unchecked guilt. Ellie can feel it.

—Do you enjoy cooking? Marla asks, retrieving a cutting board.

—I don't do much it these days, says Ellie. She watches as Marla chops a trio of carrots.

—Oh, says Marla. She bites her lip as she brushes the carrots aside, and begins to dice a pair of sweet potatoes.

—I mean, I used to. Mom and I cooked a lot, Ellie explains.

—I'm sorry, Marla replies. I didn't mean to put you on the spot.

Ellie glides her water glass across the marble, watching as ice cubes collide before slowly melting away.

—Smells like a dream, calls a man's voice from the front door. Scott hangs his jacket before meandering into the kitchen. He draws Ellie into a tight embrace, the smell of cologne lingering on his clothes.

—Merry Christmas, lil sis. I'm glad you could make it and sorry I couldn't pick you up, year end, you know? Things are crazy at the office.

—Totally, Ellie says, unsure of what to say. At times, she feels as though she barely knows him. After making his way through law school on scholarships, everything changed. They came to belong in two different worlds.

—So ... how's life? How's Jacob?

—Good, she says. What else can she say? She can't tell him they've turned the heat off, or that they haven't done laundry in a month, or that Jacob's unemployed, again.

—You working?

—Part-time. Still doing the virtual assistant stuff. It pays minimum wage and there are no guaranteed hours, but she doesn't tell him this. At least her internet is partly paid for and with time, maybe she'll save enough for a month's rent plus a security deposit in the city.

—I'm glad, he says. I don't know what you're still doing in that town, it's a dead end, you know. He tells her this as if the reality of her life has yet to hit her.

Marla hands Scott a stack of plates and points to the dining room. He arranges three circular placemats before placing the china and accompanying cutlery. The electric fireplace in the adjacent room is visible through the doorway.

—Mind turning that on? he asks.

Atop the mantle sits a trio of ribbed candles, their wicks, untouched. Next to them are photos of Scott and Marla on vacation, another of Scott and Ellie's mother when they were children, each in polished, silver frames. Ellie approaches the fireplace, skating across the laminate flooring. The soft white light of winter spilling into the living room brings with it a kind of inexplicable tranquility. For a moment, Ellie stares at the small icon, a wavering flame that will ignite the fire instantaneously. No trekking into the woods, no fumbling with kindling. Just the push of a button. She clicks it, anticipating fire, its spellbinding sway. The log set erupts with colour, suddenly cloaked in yellow, white and a reddish-orange. At first, Ellie cannot quite pinpoint what feels off. The flames are no longer as unpredictable; they are stable, eternal, the opposite of fire which is meant to die. This isn't how she'd remembered the fireplace. Instead, she is reminded of Jacob. There's nothing quite like it, he'd said, pulling her near, scooting her towards the warmth of a fire they'd built, something they earned. It's not to say that Ellie is displeased at the moment. She admits, the warmth is desirable.

The ease, even more so. But for the first time, she can't help but concede, something in her has changed. Perhaps she'll never settle for adversity the way Jacob has, she won't idealize her own misfortune, but if this life is hers, she will take from it what she can. Even if, for now, that is nothing more than the mesmerizing flames of a real fire.

• • •

Emma is a communications professional and writer based in Calgary, Alberta. With a Bachelor of Arts in History and Creative Writing from the University of Calgary, she is committed to leveraging her skills to help advance a just, deliberate and sustainable energy transition. When she is not working, Emma can be found bouldering or adventuring with her husband and their dog, Georgia.

A FALSE EXODUS
The mark-making of leaving, etched on copper plates printed on Japanese paper, cut and Chine-collé on cotton rag paper that is hand-embossed with cracks found in the institution, 2022, 48.3 x 33 cm.

Katie Bruce

STATEMENT

During the height of the programming for the Energy Futures portfolio, faculty at my university were locked out. For six weeks we walked a picket line, fighting a policy central to the Alberta United Conservative Party (UCP): to do more with less. The project became inextricably linked to an inhospitable present which threatened the potential of a greener future, one positioned by creatives and intellectuals thinking beyond known solutions. In 2020, as the pandemic reared its ugly head, the UCP invested $7,000,000,000 in a pipeline that would ultimately fail the following year; a pipe dream that oil and gas would remain relevant in a world navigating political and climate extremes. Public-serving industries were attacked with slashed budgets and performance-based funding. Critical thinking and a liberal arts education are no longer valid metrics under neoliberal policies that

turn social programs into capitalist ventures dependent on exceeding Key Performance Indicators. It is
easier to control those not raised to question what
else is possible. Members at my picketing line talked
about leaving to escape the governance that brought
us to this juncture. Ministers resigned; countless others exited silently, taking their creative and intellectual
energy with them. I cannot help but think, however,
that it was a false exodus. That the desire to escape
was misguided in believing other governments would
reject similar policies; a secret place where the public
is not a chronic customer. Did they find greener pas-
tures? Or more of the same?

• • •

*Katie Marie Bruce is a printmaker, artist, and instructor at the
University of Lethbridge in the Faculty of Fine Arts. Her current
body of research-creation looks to combine feminist readings of
Object Orientated Ontology with images of the female nude
that challenge notions of the muse as a consumable object of
desire, materially articulated in a series of copperplate etchings
and stained glass panels.*

Contemplation of the Muses—Tide Rising, Stan Phelps. Etching.
Artist's statement is at the end of this chapter.

CHAPTER FOURTEEN

CARBUNCLE

Peter Midgley, Author
Stan Phelps, Artist

CARBUNCLE THE CLOWN rides down from his perch on the ocean-front high-rise where he has juggled vigil all night. He weaves through the traffic and the throngs. In the distance, he can see the old schoolhouse, long since abandoned; the streets leading from the schoolyard into the suburbs have emptied as the people throng to the beachfront to watch the slick descend. And still the Muses sit, resplendent in their nakedness. "Go home!" Carbuncle yells as he pedals past them. "Disaster approaches!" But they do not listen. No one listens to clowns anymore.

Cars crowd the boulevard as Carbuncle the Clown makes his way toward the abandoned school where he has made his home. In the streets beyond the oceanfront, the ones that have not been swallowed by the sludge, people have gathered to film their impending doom. Carbuncle moves in the opposite direction, inland, toward the mountains, where he hopes he will be safe. During the endless recession that preceded the deluge, survivors had broken curfew at night to gather anything of use—tables and chairs; beds from the school's infirmary. The clothing pupils had left behind as they fled the wall of tailings formed a dike near the entrance. When he arrives at his home, Carbuncle clambers over the dike, dragging his unicycle with him. "One cannot be too careful in these times," he reminds himself. Where the ceiling had collapsed as a result of the underground reverberations, Carbuncle rifles through the rubble. Treasures hidden in the rafters have fallen like manna from heaven here, too.

In another life, a different life before the deluge, Carbuncle had been an echo tech. He liked, then, to think of himself as a front-line worker. He recalls how one day he had to see a newborn who was isolated for possible infection. He was used to occasionally dressing up to sound patients for potential or confirmed disease, but the experience of watching the child struggling to breathe as he himself struggled for air—two desperate bodies circling each other in a tango of death—remained with him still. He had entered the tiny negative pressure room overheated from the extra protective gear. He wore two layers of masks for his own protection, and the baby's. Halfway through his imaging routine, he realized that he was subconsciously trying not to breathe too much. For a moment, his head had spun, and he almost passed out. As he breathes rhythmically now to recover from his journey and from climbing over the rubble to get to his abode, Carbuncle recalls how he tried to focus on breathing while he was in the little room, but how the double mask he was wearing made the feeling of claustrophobia worse. He remembers too, as he picks a discarded mask off the ground, how the pressurized mask sucked into his face, making the work of breathing significant. Even though he knew better then, he caught himself subconsciously moving his jaw to create a gap and sneak in some outside air. The air he now breathes freely even as he knows it is killing him.

As he left the room with the newborn that day, Carbuncle remembers thinking, "I cannot sleep or stop my hands from shaking. As soon as the sun rises, I too will leave this place."

And yet, here he is still, guarding the grotesquerie that spreads out before him. After the incident with the newborn, Carbuncle had left the hospital and found residence in the abandoned schoolroom. He has not left the city, as he had planned to do, but returns to the schoolroom every night. He considers it his novitiate's cell, one he has chosen for himself as he searches for redemption.

Once in the school building, Carbuncle follows protocol. He washes himself down thoroughly in the cleansing room. Then he heads down the hallway to the schoolroom where he sleeps. The souls of the dead sit along the walls: Carbuncles. Just like the one attached to his own nose. The one that had grown after the incident with the child. He touches his carbuncle. It feels as though it houses the sadness of this world. It sleeps there on his nose, but when it wakes in the morning, it extends its one remaining wheel and rides beneath him on his daily rounds, obedient as a dog on a leash. It was this pet boil that had given him the name Carbuncle, by which he is now known.

When Carbuncle awakes, he repeats his resolve to leave before he and his carbuncle set out on their daily rounds. Carbuncle and his carbuncle are responsible for gathering bodies from the streets, like prayers. As the sun sets, Carbuncle returns to the schoolyard with a carbuncle full of bodies. When he returns from his volunteer shift keeping the Muses company on the oceanfront high-rises, before he goes to bed in the schoolroom, Carbuncle removes the bodies he collected during the day. He does so with care, one at a time, placing a tick beside the names of those he can still recognize from among the faces on the wall. Then he tosses the remains in the pit where the swimming pool once was.

Together, on this last morning on the day of his renewed resolve, Carbuncle and his carbuncle move through the city. The houses sit on the roadside like hermitages. Abandoned prayer cells. At the entrance to each cell, Carbuncle pauses and cries "Bring out your dead!" Then he steps back to a safe distance. When he hears no sound, he reaches his bony arm through the bars and scrapes their remains onto the shovel he holds in his other hand.

Carbuncle's once muscular body has faded. He is nothing but a tall string of snot now, little more than an arsehole propped up by two planks. All his energy has gone into dragging his load along the muddy streets every day. Carbuncle spreads his cadaverous limbs out and scrapes another body off the porch as he passes. He squeezes it into the gaping maw of the carbuncle that rolls beneath him. In the crypts of that amoeboid growth, this newest body joins the rattle of the deceased.

A woman on the porch cautions him. "Stay back—ten feet!" She tosses a small coin at him. It plops as it disappears into the caverns of his carbuncle. He feels it sink to the bottom like a coin in a wishing well.

Carbuncle feels himself seep onto the roadway, leaving a trail of yellow snot on the tar. As the sun sets, Carbuncle the Clown prepares to return to the schoolyard with his carbuncle full of bodies. Then he remembers his resolve, and instead of return-ing to his volunteer post to watch the slick glistening in the sun-set, Carbuncle rides up the hilltop behind the schoolyard. From that dizzying height, he peers through his eyelashes. He sees his carbuncle detach itself from his body and roll back toward the schoolyard. Carbuncle the Clown watches it seep along the walls before he too rises and follows it from a safe distance. Carbuncle's carbuncle lolls ahead of him, then stops.

As Carbuncle approaches it, his carbuncle looms over him like the rising sun—a sprawling, writhing mass bursting at its seams, threatening to engulf him. The main festering bulb has spawned numerous growths along the adjoining streets—those are not people he sees, but a proliferation of carbuncles, tiny oil spills glistening in the moonlight. There they sit like small shop-ping centres.

Carbuncle hesitates, then abandons his companion of many years and wanders the festering streets. He makes his way to the edge of the city. Around him, everything is awash with effluent. A body swings from a solitary tree, the knife still sticking out of its chest. Carefully, Carbuncle the Clown pulls the knife out and cuts the rope. He takes the solitary Muse down carefully and lays her down, arms folded.

As he rounds the corner, he notices a bony finger protruding from new, moonlit boil by the roadside. As Carbuncle hobbles along the outskirts of the town, heading for the hills, a shower of yellow tulips scatters from the boil, onto the road. They bow toward the spot where the Muse lies. Carbuncle does not stop his flight, nor does he look back to admire the flowers, but as he walks, he thinks: Still, despite everything, the arrival of spring.

• • •

Peter Midgley has advocated for local writers and for diversity across the writing and publishing industry. He has served as a board member and as a jury member on numerous arts organizations and has mentored and supported many local artists. He offers workshops on writing, editing and creativity. Peter has been recognized internationally for his work, which appears in print and non-traditional venues (e.g., as guerilla poetry and graffiti in Palestine's West Bank). In total, Peter has written 18 books and plays.

Stan Phelps with his the etching *Contemplation of the Muses.*

CONTEMPLATION OF THE MUSES—TIDE RISING
Etching, 2022, 48.3 x 33 cm.

Stan Phelps

STATEMENT

An all-consuming wave engulfs the developed world as the Muses, symbolizing creative freedom, contemplate our demise.

Amid the chaos, the jester derides our ambitions.

This intaglio etching pictures a dream world and the incongruous manifestations of the psyche.

The harlequin/jester mocks our preoccupation with monumentalizing achievements, while the earth reclaims its own.

The tsunami symbolizes the ultimatum that we face with respect to the exploitation of the planet and our dire need to find alternative sources of energy.

The image originated as an oil painting, followed by the etching, which was printed at the Heart Studio in Calgary, Alberta.

• • •

Stan Phelps, a Calgarian, is a painter, printmaker, muralist, designer, and art educator. Stan has worked at several internationally renowned art studios and is a founding member of the Alberta Printmakers' Society. He is represented in the Canada Council Art Bank, the Alberta Foundation for the Arts, La Biblioteque Nationale and in private and corporate art collections.

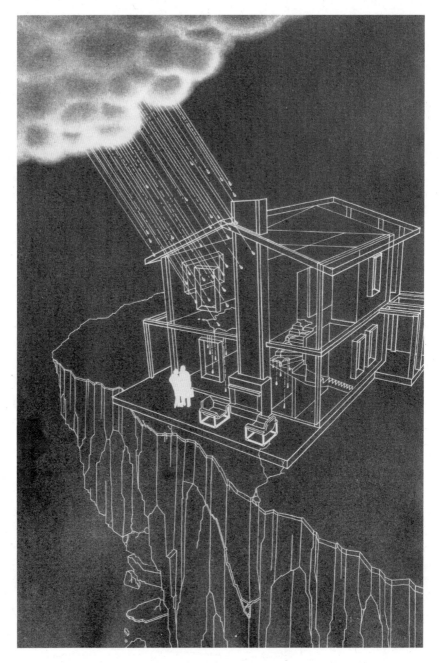

Model Homes, Jill Ho-You. Cyanotype.
Artist's statement is at the end of this chapter.

CHAPTER FIFTEEN

LAST BREATH

Mark Hopkins, Author
Jill Ho-You, Artist

LAST BREATH

"Extinction," she whispers, "isn't a question of if, but when."

She smiles wryly, inhales humanity's last breath, and then... that's it. The story goes on without us.

Except, of course, that's not how she dies. That's the Disney version, polished, philosophical, satisfying. We don't know how it ends. But it's probably messy. It's probably soon.

A hundred years from now, let's say. She's the great-grandchild of someone alive today. She's old enough, barely, to remember when weather reports came without death counts; old enough to remember weather reports. She's old enough to remember air conditioning, and money, and suburbs, and so many other things that used to seem important.

When she was younger, and had someone to talk to, she said things like, "It's not the end of the world," things like, "Humans are parasites, the world's better off without us." And, sure, it might be. After the last mass extinction, ecosystems bounced back in thirty million years or so. Mammals did well, last time. Why not roll the dice again? Will the next dominant species cure diseases? Write poetry?

As she trekked through bone-dry forests, haunted by the bodies she left behind in the city, as she survived on emaciated rabbits, as starving insects survived on her, it was easier to think about everything the world would gain when humanity was gone, rather than everything lost.

She outlasts all the rest, everyone who fried in the sun, everyone swept away in roaring floodwaters, everyone killed with smart bombs and desperate guns. She survives the plagues, the new ones and the tenacious opportunists. She survives the fires. The hurricanes. The freezing rain. The hunger. The thirst. She survives the cascade of overlapping apocalypses, until she doesn't.

And then... that's it. The human story, spanning three hundred thousand years, ends with her last breath, exhaled after a life of hardship on a scorched planet.

It doesn't have to go like this.

If we choose differently now, if we act urgently, we could be at the beginning of the human story, instead of its conclusion. Humanity's last breath could be breathed, not in a century's time, but in a distant future.

Three million years from now, let's say. She's the great (x100,000)-grandchild of someone alive today.

She learned about Earth in a history book, about those fleeting, deluded centuries when we thought everything could be a factory—farms, hospitals, schools, all conveyor belts of manufactured progress. She learned about how we teetered right on the edge of self-destruction, and the rallying efforts it took to pull us back into right relations.

She was Homo sapiens, but hardly thought she was the last. The branching of species had been underway for millennia, and sapiens the minority for centuries. If her bones were a little denser, her retinas a little less sensitive, it didn't make her stand out at parties, didn't impede her research into ancient solar technologies, her work on high-efficiency energy conversion for isolated communities.

When the documentary crew asked to feature her in a series called "The Last Human," she consented with surprise and curiosity. Later, it made her a little sad. She liked the aspirational quality of Homo sapiens, "wise human". Plus, being the last of her species felt... a bit weird. A bit lonely.

She dies in bed, a gentle end, in the care of not-quite-humans (as similar to us as we were to Neanderthals), surrounded by her not-quite-human children and grandchildren. She dies after days of nostalgic stories, of smiles, tears and goodbyes, of her great-grandchild crawling into a sunbeam and cooing when it hits their face.

When the news spreads, some people mutter "Good riddance, filthy apes" because, no matter the species, hominids are hominids. Others, though, pause to ponder the end of an era, a few million years of coincidence and courage and narrowly averted calamity, leading to... this. A star-spanning species, still (always) imperfect but ever-more in harmony with the workings of the universe.

This not-quite-human species will come to an end, too; they all do. Extinction isn't a question of if, but when. But every year it's pushed back is another year of joy and pain, of discovery and adventure, of hardship and triumph and love. Every new year means that people yesterday worked and fought and strived for people tomorrow, made choices with their well-being and well-becoming in mind.

Someday, the human story will end. Together, day by day, year by year, choice by choice, we decide how our story will unfold.

THE END OF ALBERTA

Part 1: We did it!

Francis Fukuyama said history was over. I believed him.

I would've just turned six years old when his famous essay, "The End of History?", was published in 1989; I was nine when his follow-up book, The End of History and the Last Man came out. In them, Fukuyama proposed that, following the end of the Cold War, humanity was witnessing the "universalization of Western liberal democracy as the final form of human government".

As a child, I didn't read the essay or the book. I probably didn't even know they existed, unless some grown-up mentioned them at a dinner party. But I lived in the world that Fukuyama described. I was a comfortably upper-middle-class white boy, nestled in the assurances of free markets and liberal democracies, my future assured in prosperous Alberta. History was a thing that had happened to other people.

Meanwhile, history—of course—was unfolding all around me. The Kanehsatà:ke Resistance, Tiananmen Square, the U.S. invasion of Panama, the LA riots, cholera and yellow fever epidemics, the HIV/AIDS pandemic, wars in Bosnia, Iraq, Iran, Kuwait, Somalia, Yemen. All, shamefully, felt like bumps in the road, growing pains as the world settled into its glorious future path. The story I happily accepted was one of walls falling, dictatorships crumbling, wars ending, cures for diseases, civil rights triumphs, astonishing technological development, and a glowing future. I was living in a bubble, my thinking limited by my narrow context. All the good, none of the bad.

With one major exception.

Growing up, I spent nearly every summer at Skeleton Lake in Ontario. One of my most cherished memories is of stepping out into the clear, shallow water to see the sandy bottom dotted with tadpoles. As my summer vacation unfolded, I watched the tadpoles sprout legs, watched their tails slowly shrink until, after a few short weeks, they had completed their transformation into frogs. But, as we returned in subsequent summers, there were fewer and fewer of them. After fifteen years, where there had once been seemingly endless fields of tadpoles, I struggled to spot even one or two.

There are many possible culprits. The chytrid fungus ravaging amphibian populations around the world, spread by human trade and travel, doesn't seem to have severely impacted Canada yet, but there's habitat destruction and seeping toxins as new roads, homes and factories are built, warmer weather drying up ponds, shifting breeding seasons and weakening immune systems, or (likely) some insidious combination of all these and more.

And it wasn't just the tadpoles; it was coral reefs dying, bumblebees disappearing, forests burning, global warming. If my worldview was one of unceasing human progress, it was playing out on a backdrop of ecological destruction. While these two perspectives were seemingly dissonant and incompatible, they both supported the idea that history was over. If the first was, "Hey everyone, we did it, we've sorted out the perfect political system and now we get to relax," the second was, "Hey everyone, we did it, we've devastated our biosphere beyond any hope of repair and now we're marching to our doom."

Inevitable progress, or inevitable catastrophe. Neither offered the possibility of meaningful change, or of agency to make change. Both were convincing, compelling... and, ultimately, wrong. History isn't over, and the choices we're making right now matter more than ever.

Part 2: Booming and zooming

I was born in Calgary in 1983. By that point, Alberta's transformation into a petrostate had been underway for decades, properly kicked off when Imperial Oil drilled its fateful well near Leduc in 1947, about four years before my parents were born. The subsequent boom drew my parents out west from Ontario in the late seventies, not dissuaded by bumper stickers shouting, "Let the Eastern bastards freeze in the dark." My dad, with his geophysical engineering degree, landed a job with Shell after his first interview. Over the next few years, as my parents got settled, Alberta's festering sense of Western alienation swelled with the creation of Pierre Trudeau's National Energy Program in 1980... but, while the resentment is still strong to this day, the recession that prompted the NEP was already fading when I came into the world.

By the time I started school, Alberta was booming again, a roaring boom that seemed like it would never end. As I grew up, Calgary's office towers rose higher and its suburbs sprawled wider. For decades, people flocked to Alberta for paycheques and bonuses, and the boom kept on booming right through to 2015, when I was thirty-two years old. That year, the global price of oil tanked and Alberta's economy went down with it, starkly exposing the province's over-dependency on a resource in decline.

In the broad sweep of time, thirty-two years is barely a blip—but humans don't live for very long. Assuming I make it to old age, I spent a third of my life, including my formative years, in an Alberta flush with oil cash, under a Progressive Conservative government whose reign seemed like it would never end. No wonder the world felt unchanging and unchangeable, and that the events of 2015—when the boom busted and the PCs were toppled—came as a shock.

If I had zoomed out a bit more, though, I may have seen hints that my "normal" was anything but.

For instance—I might have been less surprised by the Alberta NDP's election win in 2015 if I had looked more closely into the name of my high school. I knew that "Bible Bill", the namesake of William Aberhart High, had been a preacher and radio host, but I knew nothing about the Social Credit Party that he led to victory in 1935, and that acted as Alberta's "natural governing party" until it was dislodged in 1971 by Peter Lougheed's Progressive Conservatives. By the time I was old enough to vote, the PCs had been in power for thirty years, nearly twice my lifespan, and it seemed like the only way to meaningfully participate in provincial democracy was to buy a PC membership and vote in their leadership race (which I did, multiple times). But, just like Social Credit, the PCs were only inevitable until they weren't.

Zoom out further, and even the hypercapitalism that I was born into, and that was embraced with triumphant enthusiasm in the halls of those soaring office towers, has only dominated our world since the 1970s. While this "winners take all" financial philosophy and the extreme inequality it fosters have been launched to new heights by globalization, it's a story we've seen —and refuted—before, with the guillotines of France's Reign of Terror or the busting of Gilded Age railroad monopolies in the United States.

Zoom out further still, and I'd see that the arbitrary borders of so-called "Alberta" were drawn barely more than a century ago. All the oil booms and busts, the political dynasties, the fortunes made and lost, are the blink of an eye compared to the tens of thousands of years that Indigenous peoples have lived on these lands, learning and shifting and changing in deep alignment with the dynamic ecosystems in which we're all embedded, that have evolved over millions of years.

The realities I saw as permanent and immutable were all so recent, so clearly constructed and fleeting that—when I finally did zoom out—I felt silly to have mistaken these slivers of reality for the whole thing.

But zooming out is hard. Our lives are short. Our lives are full. We forget.

I was lucky. My parents, "Laurentian Elites" from hated Ontario, never fully bought into Alberta's petrostate propaganda; even as I grew up immersed in it, home was a place where its tightly held truths could be questioned. Then, during that endless boom, I stumbled into an arts career, and I started volunteering, and I met more and more people that hadn't bought into the myth of inevitable progress because they'd been left out of it—prosperous Alberta was never prosperous for everyone. And slowly, as my context expanded, my view of the world grew—and continues to grow—ever larger.

Much as my narrow context limited my thinking, that same narrow thinking is perhaps our biggest challenge in Alberta today. Too often, living here and watching the state of business and politics, I find myself wanting to scream, "Fuck your profits, your wealth, your quarterly reports; fuck your politics, your job, your hurt feelings, your ideologies; don't you fucking understand that we're going to die, and you're killing us?"

The "you" receiving my outrage is often hard to pin down; the blame for the climate crisis is distributed. I may not be an oil executive, but I'm complicit in my own ways. And given how powerfully the stories of progress and prosperity captured me, I can only imagine how much stronger they must resonate for someone whose career, family's future and identity are wrapped up in the "conventional" energy sector. As Upton Sinclair so aptly pointed out, it's difficult to get someone to understand something when their salary depends upon their not understanding it.

So, I get it. I'm grateful for the opportunities I've had in Alberta, too. And change is hard, especially when it's a change of mindset, ideology, or worldview, especially when the status quo has been working for you. But we do need to change. Fast. On our current trajectory, it won't just be the Eastern bastards freezing in the dark. It'll be all of us: freezing, burning, starving, dying.

Part 3: Goldilocks
When I think about energy transition, I think about extinction. Here's why.

Homo sapiens evolved about 300,000 years ago during the Pleistocene—an Ice Age. Up to thirty percent of the planet was covered in glaciers and our hunter-gatherer ancestors, when they ventured forth from equatorial Africa, learned how to survive harsh, frigid winters as they journeyed across Asia and into the Americas.

About eleven thousand years ago, the world started to warm up. The milder, stable climate of the Holocene created the conditions for agriculture, for population growth, for cities—everything we now recognize as "civilization". All our written histories come from this Goldilocks era, not too hot, not too cold, just right for humans.

Then we started to burn coal, and gas, and oil. This transition away from photosynthetic energy (the power of plants, animals, wood and labour) to carbon-based energy led to previously unimaginable growth in human wealth, population, lifespan and innovation. We kept digging and shipping and burning, at ever greater scales, pumping hundreds of millions of years of sequestered carbon into the air at a frenetic pace, driving the global average atmospheric carbon dioxide to 421 parts per million by 2022, the highest it's been in fourteen million years. It's still climbing.

That's a problem.

It's a problem that is now well-understood—but stubbornly resisted by some. Carbon dioxide and other "greenhouse gases" help trap the Sun's energy in Earth's atmosphere as heat. Usually, atmospheric changes are gradual, unfolding over thousands or millions of years. Our feverish, relentless burning is pumping greenhouse gases into the atmosphere a hundred times faster than any recorded natural process. And the more we burn, the hotter Earth gets.

We're a remarkable species in many ways. Perhaps our most tragic distinction is that we're the first single species to bring a geologic epoch to an end. To put it simply: the Holocene was a boom for humanity. The Anthropocene, our current and eponymous epoch, is on track to be the biggest bust we've ever seen.

Our species evolved in a cold world and thrived in a mild one. Never, in the whole history of our species, have we lived on a hot planet. And sure, we're adaptable, we're scrappy, maybe some of us will find a way through. But it's worth remembering—by the end of the Ice Age, before the dawn of agriculture, the global human population was only a few hundred thousand. Now, there are more than eight billion of us. If our agricultural systems fail in a radically altered climate, we may not go extinct, but the death toll will be monstrous.

The current conversation around energy transition is often polarized, and a shorthand for the debate is "Burn, baby, burn" (for advocates of continued fossil fuel development) on one side, versus "Leave it in the ground" (for advocates of ceasing fossil fuel development) on the other. I often encounter people who are distressed by this polarization, who want to find a more nuanced middle between the extremes.

Yes, polarization is a huge problem that clouds the public conversation and slows decision-making. And yes, energy transition is far too complex to be captured in simplistic binaries. But politics aside, the laws of thermodynamics and the likelihood of human survival land much closer to one side of this argument... and it's not the side that wants to keep stoking the flames.

When I think about energy transition, I think about extinction because our survival is at stake. Our actions over the past few centuries have triggered the planet's sixth mass extinction, and the thousands of species that have already been lost are a tragedy beyond reckoning. Right now, we need to do everything in our power to avoid joining their ranks.

Part 4: Short lives, long stories

Francis Fukuyama never said history was over. I misquoted him. "The end of history" was a phrase he borrowed from German philosopher Georg Wilhelm Friedrich Hegel who, in the wake of the French Revolution, proposed that the end point history is trending toward is liberal democracy. Writing at the end of the Cold War, Fukuyama agreed.

He's still convinced. In October 2022, he published an article titled "More Proof That This Really Is the End of History" in The Atlantic. "This", in the title, refers to liberal democracy... but damn, for someone already inclined to believe that the future is fixed, and nothing we do matters, that is a very easy title to misinterpret. When something confirms your existing beliefs, it's seductively tempting to not dig any deeper.

Whether or not you buy Fukuyama's "end of history"—and

I'm not sure that I do—importantly, he doesn't see liberal democracy's global adoption as inevitable or passive. In the face of recent setbacks and reversals, he says, "Liberal democracy will not make a comeback unless people are willing to struggle on its behalf." On that point, I fervently agree. We can substitute "liberal democracy" for any desired future: we will not build circular economies, renewable energy systems, a just, anti-oppressive and decolonized society, unless people are willing to struggle on their behalf.

The challenge of the climate crisis is huge. The struggle can feel futile. But there are many reasons to believe it's not.

The story of progress I happily accepted in my youth wasn't all wrong. The strides that have been made over recent decades and centuries in human health, human rights, ecological stewardship, scientific inquiry, greater equality, equity and justice, and so much more are truly extraordinary. I just missed the fact that these triumphs were far from linear or guaranteed. Behind them, there were countless organizers, advocates and coalitions, mobilizations, riots and revolutions, setbacks, reversals and tragedies.

Progress on the climate crisis, on energy transition, is no different. And the good news, as Chris Turner points out in the foreword to this volume, is that "we are in fact moving very, very fast" to tackle these challenges.

We don't know—we can't know—if our efforts will be fast enough, deep enough, wide enough. One thing, though, is clear: if we do nothing, we're fucked. The only way to know if these crises can be mitigated, if a vibrant future for humanity is possible, is if we try with every ounce of our beings, with every tool at our disposal, with everything we've got.

People often ask Dr. Ayana Elizabeth Johnson, a marine biologist and climate policy expert, what they can do to help address the climate crisis. In a TED Talk titled "How to Find Joy in Climate Action", she calls on each of us to activate our special talents, our "superpowers", to help build the future we so desperately need.

She suggests drawing a Venn diagram to map three questions: What are you good at? What is the work that needs doing? What brings you joy? "The goal," she says, "is to be at the heart of this Venn diagram for as many minutes of your life as you can."

Our lives are short, but they matter. We aren't helpless supporting characters, swept up in the story of humanity. We are authors. As we write our own life stories, they help shape how that broader story will unfold.

I want the story of future Alberta to include solar panels on every roof and wind turbines spread across the horizon. I want to see grasslands dotted with bison, a keystone species restored. I want to see agriculture that's regenerative and flourishing, fields of permaculture free of orphan wells. I want to see holistic communities, with cheap and green and plentiful electricity, bike paths connected to local markets, and good homes for all. I want to see the same kind of wild innovation that created brilliant but destructively extractive technologies, like steam-assisted gravity drainage, turn its focus to smart grids, energy storage, carbon capture, to technologies that restore the natural world rather than ravaging it. I want to see Indigenous resurgence, and the forging of right relations between settlers on this land and its first peoples. I want to see an Alberta that doesn't set itself apart from the world, but that plays its part in a connected humanity, striving to do better.

Some of that's underway. Some of it isn't. And all of it, every part of that dream, has forces working actively in opposition.

Whatever Alberta we want to see, whatever world we want to see... it's not just going to happen. It will take work, often work that won't show results in our lifetimes, the work of generations. It will take us.

Change is possible, but not inevitable.

We can change. Let's.

Recommended Resources

Fukuyama, Francis. "More Proof That This Really Is the End of History." *The Atlantic*, October 2022.

Johnson, Ayana Elizabeth. "How to Find Joy in Climate Action." TED, June 2022. www.ted.com/talks/ayana_elizabeth_johnson_how_to_find_joy_in_climate_action

Krenak, Ailton. *Ideas to Postpone the End of the World*. House of Anansi Press, 2020.

Piketty, Thomas. *A Brief History of Equality*. The Belknap Press of Harvard University Press, 2022.

Scranton, Roy. *Learning to Die in the Anthropocene: Reflections on the End of a Civilization*. City Lights Books, 2015.

Smil, Vaclav. *Energy and Civilization: A History*. The MIT Press, 2017.

Turner, Chris. *The Patch: The People, Pipelines, and Politics of the Oil Sands*. Simon & Schuster, 2018.

• • •

Mark Hopkins is Artistic Director of Swallow-a-Bicycle Theatre, which generates productive discomfort through art, and an Associate with Human Venture Leadership, which helps build our collective capacities to reduce ignorance, error, waste, suffering and injustice. He also works with Inside Out Theatre, Kawalease Arab Canadian Theatre and the Centre for Newcomers, and is a Fellow with the Energy Futures Lab.

MODEL HOMES
Cyanotype, 2022, 48.3 x 33 cm.

Jill Ho-You

STATEMENT

My work examines the ways in which we perceive and attempt to cope with our current state of environmental precarity. Evidence that human-driven environmental damage has far-reaching and recurring negative effects has been central to debates regarding global warming and large-scale natural resource extraction operations. Recognition in the natural sciences that we have entered the "Anthropocene," an epoch caused by increased industrial, agricultural, and technological advances - has furthered the speculation into the unforeseen ramifications of our influence on the environment and ultimately the viability of humankind. Using abstracted industrial, architectural, and geological imagery, my work attempts to confront the anxiety and fear we have about the future of the planet by imaging the world if the Anthropocene culminates in uninhabitable climate change, shrinking biodiversity, and unsustainability.

• • •

Jill Ho-You is an Associate Professor in Print Media at the Alberta University of the Arts. Her practice explores the intersection of trauma, embodied memory, and the environment through print media, bioArt and installation. Her work has been exhibited internationally, including solo exhibitions at the University of the Arts in Philadelphia and The New Gallery in Calgary, AB.

Transition Prism—Fireflies Facet, Eveline Kolijn.
Etching, constructed into a prism.
Artist's statement is at the end of this chapter.

CHAPTER SIXTEEN

FIREFLIES

Uchechukwe Peter Umezurike, Author
Eveline Kolijn, Artist

DON'T KNOW how long I have lived in the Commune. Let's say it's been a week. Maybe two days. There is no clock or calendar in the buildings, so no one keeps track of time. Half of the world's problems started with the human desire to control, manipulate, and exploit time. That's what Lotem, one of the Guides, told me when I'd asked her what day it was.

Everything is *supposed* to be simple, she said.

Yet there is nothing simple about the Commune. Or how the Guides run it. It is a place of marvel, that's all I can say until my head clears.

From all that soot, I guess. My throat feels a little itchy.

Tired of asking for the time or date, I converted the notebook on my desk into a journal. I don't know what month, week, or day it is, so I start with my birth month: January 11.

January 10

The day before I start journaling. I didn't know how I got here at first because I'd passed out from the soot. When I came to, I saw four or five people standing around me. They introduced themselves as the Guides, a group that runs this strange place in the middle of nowhere.

If my memory is to be trusted, January 10 was the day Lotem showed me around the Commune. I'd slept deeply for two days, and when I woke up on the third day, the reek of fumes in my nostrils, I suddenly remembered the people in yellow overalls, goggles, masks, and helmets. I later learned they were the Salvagers, individuals who worked in devastated environments around the world, rescuing hundreds of children.

Lotem had just finished pointing out the various sections in the Commune. We were leaving the Relaxation Den when I saw some children across from us. They sat behind desks scribbling in notebooks. I'd never seen people of different colours gathered in one place, working together as if of one mind and purpose.

A few of them looked up, smiled, and waved at us. Lotem said they'd been living here for some time. I lifted my hand but didn't wave nor smile because my chest hurt, and my eyes dripped now and then.

"What is this area called?" I spoke for the first time since Lotem began the section tour.

"Oh, that." Her eyes sparkled. "The Imagination Den!"

"The what?"

She said it again.

"They're taking a quiz or what?"

Lotem laughed. "You'd be surprised how much the Commune has benefited from the children's imagination. Actually," she drew out her words, "they are imagining the future."

"What future?" I scoffed. "Is there any left?"

Lotem regarded me as if slightly taken aback.

I glanced at my nails, blackened from the soot. I had to find my way out of this place. Figure out how to find my mother, wherever she may be.

"Come on, Gozzy," Lotem finally said, tugging me gently by the wrist. "Let's get you back to your room."

January 12
Thinking about loss only makes it more painful. I have already lost my father. I can't think of loss yet again. My mother had to have made it out of Soot City.

January 13
From the corner of my eye, I see Lotem drawing closer. Tall, soft-spoken, and patient. She often stops briefly to chat when she sees me gazing out the window. I don't think she ever feels offended, even when I ignore her.

I find her voice soothing, like that of a nurse. And she is always calm, like she wouldn't even scream if a wind snatched her and tossed her around the place. She reminds me of my mother: fearless.

But now I drift away from the window, slip down the hallway, and into my room, avoiding her.

January 14
The Guides encourage every child to mingle. They worry I am getting lost in myself, that the loss, coupled with loneliness, may scar my mind. I'm grateful to stay in the Commune, not to have to breathe the blackened air again, but I should be looking for my mother.

January 15
None of us children know which part of the world the Commune is located, no Guide will tell us. If you ask, they say it does not matter. What matters is that we are here—we have one another and together, we can reimagine our world, whatever that means.

January 16
The Commune does feel like a prison, but it's a sanctuary. We follow routines, but not strictly. The Guides say we're free to leave anytime, but no one is brave enough to venture past

the perimeters. People sometimes eat out on the deck, on the lawn, or in the cafeteria.

This afternoon, while eating some mashed potatoes, sweet corns, and peas, I hear a girl mention, "Behemoths." I suddenly remember my mother saying that someone didn't want my father producing cheaper hydropanels that extracted water from the atmosphere.

Then, one evening, a freak explosion had happened at the research facility while he had been testing another set of hydropanels.

January 17

It is too late—Lotem has appeared behind me just as I am about to escape. Though I'm still afraid since the city is covered in soot and parents are missing.

Frowning, I look up at her. She doesn't understand what is happening outside the Commune. Or maybe she does but thinks it is not much serious. She has not watched adults clutching their chests and children choking in the street.

Lotem rests her hand on my shoulder. She hasn't lost anyone, I suspect. Though fourteen, I'm old enough to know it is useless to hope.

January 18

A crescent moon hangs in the sky. I lie in bed wondering how long it took them to build the Commune, whose idea it was in the first place, how they have managed not to run out of food, water, and electricity. How long will all this last? How did the Commune escape the crisis happening worldwide?

Everything around here looks unreal, like something out of a fantastic movie. The rooms are compact and built with recycled wine corks, bark sidings, and plastic. I'm amazed that everyone has a room with a toilet and bath to themselves. How did the Guides put all this together? Did they know there'd be a need for such a place someday?

Maybe I'll wake up one day and find that I've been living in a soot-induced dream.

January 20

At the window, I watch some boys chase after a ball across the field. Girls toss frisbees amongst themselves. Others hang around the swings and slides; a few children sit on the grass chatting. There are dogs running after each other and cats lounging around people. Blue sky, white clouds, and the air smells of lavender blossoms. Nothing feels polluted around here. Too tempting to think that the world is sunny and fine like this outside the Commune walls.

Birch, maple, marula, linden, sycamore, and cedar trees fringe the perimeters like guards. A colourful book called *Caring for Trees.* During my rest time, I try to memorize their names. It's a miracle that they still have vegetation here.

Every now and then, a squirrel darts out of a shrub. A few robins, blue jays, and chickadees zip from one tree to another. There's also a book, *Bird Ethics, in the Knowledge Den, a library and museum of sorts, that I've been reading.*

The last time I saw birds, they dropped by the hundreds from the sky.

January 21

Fifty or seventy children arrive monthly in the Commune. Some are covered in blisters or wounds; others look grimy and ragged. No adults. No news of my mother yet. I watch the helicopters lift into the sky, then fade, hoping the Salvagers continue to search for survivors.

January 22

Many children seem to have accepted their losses. Or maybe they're just really good at pretending. Perhaps the longer you live in the Commune, the easier it is for you not to dwell much on the past. This is probably what gives the Guides hope.

But that's where I am different. I don't want to move on.

The Guides refuse to see that I'm different—even though some of these children don't look like me. Or speak my language. Sometimes I can't even make out some of what they say: some speak a little too fast and others rather haltingly.

The only thing we all share, I guess, is that we've lost a parent or two. Our homes remain devastated by Behemoths—a chain of global companies that extract petroleum, gold, diamond, copper, coltan, bauxite, and uranium; raze forests, drain rivers, crater lands, and dislocate humans and animals anywhere.

We are all displaced. Dispossessed.

January 24

I stand in the corner of the Creation Den, watching a cohort of teenagers fabricate an intricate device the size of a tabletop fridge.

"What are you guys working on?" I ask, unable to check my curiosity.

"It's a boiler," a boy replies.

"Oh yeah?" I say. "What is it for?"

They exchange glances.

"It is a biomass generator, which we use to combust wood, paper, food waste, and anything organic..."

"...and shit, I mean, poo," a girl chips in, with a grin.

I stare at her. Of course, I know what a biomass does.

She shrugs, then explains, "You'll see it once we've finished building it. It produces some of the energy used for cooking, heating, and charging the inverters in the Commune. This is one of the really cool things we get to build around here. Wait until you see the portable solar generators, wind turbines, fog harvesters, and heat pumps. Or even the composters. Very cool, right?"

January 25

I worry about my mother. Lotem said the Salvagers haven't been successful in their recent rescue missions. How did thousands of children survive this global environmental destruction and their parents did not?

Maybe it has something to do with our immune system.

Or pure luck.

January 26
It's been about sixteen days since I started journaling. Still no words from the Salvagers about my mother. Is she wounded? Lying under a boulder? Or limping along the mangroves where we had lost each other?

January 27
Sunbirds painted on my curtains. Unable to sleep, I remember how one night, the stars had filled the sky, fireflies danced all over the place, and the world glowed like a harvest moon. Then everyone had gone to bed. When we awoke the following day, huge shadows had devoured the sun.

Panic and darkness attacked the streets. Cars and cyclists crashed. The air stank of melting plastic and rubber, leaving the lungs scorched. People sank to their feet, gasping, coughing, and choking.

All this happened many weeks or months ago, but the images refused to fade, even slightly, from my mind.

January 29
I grudgingly join the other children in the Illumination Den, where the Guides update us about their increasing green energy capacity. They talk about what other Communes are doing. They sound pleased.

There's no leader among them; they seem to work together without friction. Or maybe they've learned to mask it well.

"All this couldn't have been possible," says one of the Guides, "without your imagination and effort. We may need to build more generators and inverters in the future, but for now, thank you. Thank you."

I catch Lotem watching me.

I stare at her without blinking.

January 30
I am splattering peanut butter on a slice of bread when I hear the freckled girl say, "We're lucky that it only took two days before the Salvagers came to our city."

"Yo, what city are you from?" asks a pimply-faced boy sitting across from me.

"The Great Slick."

"Oh, monstrous," the boy says. "I heard the pipelines exploded and flooded your villages with their spills. Yo, that is so monstrous."

The girl scoops some yogurt into her mouth, then nods. "Imagine being unable to cook for those days because everyone was terrified that we would all go up in flames. It was ghastly. The fishes and crabs didn't survive the spills."

January 31

In the last five days, over our meals, I've met fellow teenagers from various places I've heard nothing about until now. Places as far as Nigeria, Canada, Namibia, South Africa, Venezuela, Haiti, the United States, Iraq, and the Pacific Islands.

The pimply-faced boy is from Tar Land, where sludge has turned the lands and lakes black as bitumen. Another boy is from Flare Town, where the gas flares have left many residents dead. There are twin sisters from Calcified Falls, where acid rains have blanched the soils and rusted the plants. Then there is Taiye, who, like me, is from Soot City.

February 1

Taiye and I sit on the deck, watching the cobalt sky.

My mother and I used to count fireflies at night before we went to bed.

"I never noticed the stars until we left Soot City."

Her parents had died from the soot. I rub my knees. It is chilly. Still, it feels pleasant watching the calm above us. I hear some chirping in the shrubs and put a hand on her shoulder.

She rubs my hand. "You're not much of a talker."

"It's not as though we saw a lot of stars before either," I say. "Remember the flaring from the oil companies dimmed them even before the soot ever appeared."

"True. And yet, the stars have always been there for us. Life has possibilities not yet destroyed."

"I suppose we are lucky." I'm afraid we both sound like Lotem.

Taiye pins her gaze on me. "Are we?"

"Everyone here thinks so."

"I'm curious. What do you think, Gozzy?" She prods me with her elbow. "This is the future, right?"

February 2

"Hope is the action we take now," Lotem says, sitting beside me in the Relaxation Den.

"Seriously?" I roll my eyes. "That's a load of muck. You really don't believe all this talk about hope, do you?"

It takes a moment before Lotem answers. Then, finally, she inhales. "There are days that are incredibly tough, but I think hope is the last fortress we have in these times." She reaches out a hand to me. "I understand how you feel..."

"No, you don't," I snap. "Just stop it."

"Gozzy, I am so sorry."

"No, you're not." My throat stings like it had with the soot. I cross my arms. She sounds like my father, too full of hope. "You live in this whatever place you call it, and you think everything is going to be just okay? You have your fields, greenhouses, recycling plants, clean energy, and those fragile little gadgets, or whatever it is you call them. And you think this is...all...going to last? Trust me, it won't!"

I storm off to my room.

February 3

My father makes funny faces at the dinner table, but this memory hardly cheers me up. I end up feeling sore.

February 4

I stay quiet throughout breakfast, lunch, and dinner. Taiye asks if I am okay. I tell her I will be. Eventually.

February 6

"I didn't mean to snap at you, Lotem. I'm sorry for acting like a spoiled brat."

"No, Gozzy. You don't have to apologize. It's my fault."

"No, it's not. I have no right to think I've suffered more than anyone. Or get angry that almost everyone seems unaffected by what's happened beyond the Commune."

Lotem sighs. "We all suffer and deal with loss in our own way."

"It's hard to hope."

"Yes, it's hard to hope. But what's the alternative?"

"You ever get scared?"

"Yes, I get scared. Everybody does."

"I'm scared. What if...?" My mother's face blurs in my mind as my words trail off.

Lotem sucks in air. "I thought I'd never forgive myself for the death of my partner and our boys. He was an environmental activist who mobilized people to protest the fracking in the prairies. Some men came to our house one night and started shooting into our rooms. There were days I woke up hating myself and considered ending my life. But I realised that I couldn't give the murderers an easy victory. So I get what you mean. I've wrestled with that 'What if' myself."

In silence, we watch the sun go down in the distance. Patches of red, yellow, and orange in the sky. Like the sunbirds on my curtains.

February 7

The Salvagers have discovered signs of adults in underground shelters in different parts of the world. We got the news from the Guides during the updates in the Illumination Den. There is a chance my mother is still alive.

February 8

"Whoa." My eyes pop. "Where...what is this place?"

"Welcome to the Habitats." Lotem sweeps her arms grandly, like a tour guide.

No words can describe the massive, glassed domes standing before us or the small brook running through the terraces at their centre. There are five of them: three larger domes and two medium-sized ones. The domes are used to breed thousands of insects and plants, Lotem says.

"We've been doing our best to keep their population steady. Although it is a lot of work and we don't know if we will succeed, it has been worth every bit of it," she adds.

My fingers tingle. "They are beautiful."

"You should see the Habitats at sunrise, how the lights bounce off the domes, bathing them in a soft purple."

"Sunsets make everything spectacular."

"Yes, you're right. Sunsets have their own beauty. I hope one day you'll get to see the Flashing at sunrise."

"What's the Flashing?"

"That's where the fireflies live. Magical, to say the least."

I remember the last time I made a lightning bug lantern before the fireflies started to disappear. Cold light, my science teacher, Mr. Ankh, had called it in our class on bioluminescent organisms.

"I can't wait to see the fireflies."

"That's why I brought you here. But we will start with the Blooms, the Beehives, the Pollinators, the Sanctuary, and the Flashing."

February 9

My heart almost packs up. The sky looks like it's burning, but it is not—those are just giant streaks of orange, yellow, and purple. I was afraid the soot had reached the Commune.

Everyone is asleep but me. A knapsack on my back, I stand at the gate. I can slip under it and, with my flashlight, find my way in the dark. Whatever is out there doesn't scare me. I'm strong enough to survive on my own. I have six bottles of water, lots of energy and protein bars.

I only worry that my mother might come looking for me here while I've gone searching for her.

I bite my nails and creep back to my room.

February 11

Awake in bed, I think about the hundreds of fireflies in the Habitats. I've never seen such large numbers of fireflies before, let alone find them flashing synchronously in one place. Like a million tiny stars.

February 12

I visit the Habitats again. Later that night, I'd dream of my mother following a path lighted by fireflies. Yellow and green lights bounce off her hairs. She beams at me.

February 15

Today makes it the fourth time I've been to the Habitats. Yesterday, I went with Taiye to watch the fireflies. We stood there while they flickered at us.

February 18

Taiye and I sit on the deck gazing into the sunset. I want to tell her that I saw fireflies guiding my mother in my dream. Instead, I talk about how my father had developed a machine that converted hydrogen into heat.

"That's super cool."

"Yeah, I know," I say, smiling. "He was working on another project, how to extract insect fat for biodiesel production. Then..." I pause and glance down, afraid I might cry. "The soot happened, and...but he showed me how to develop photovoltaic cells."

A shadow crosses Taiye's face. Then she touches my arm. "Your dad must be a great man. I'm sure he is proud of you, wherever he is."

The domes glisten in the sunset.

I catch Taiye watching me. "What?"

"Nothing," she says, shrugging.

"Say it."

"So you are a nerd?"

"The kettle is calling the pot black. I'm sure you're the super nerd in the whole Commune."

Taiye smiles. "Hmm. I'm just eager to see you put your super brain to use. But you first have to stop looking cold and distant all the time."

Her words somehow cut deep.

February 20

In the Illumination Den, while the Guides are giving updates, a single word flashes in my head: Luminescence. I start to play with words: luminescent, luminous, lucent, lucid.

February 22

I wince at the lamplight when I wake up to pee in the middle of the night. I'd forgotten to turn it off. Save energy, I remind myself after I finish peeing. Mr. Ankh's voice suddenly comes alive as I crawl back into bed: *The firefly has a lamp. It has an enzyme known as Luciferase and a molecule known as Luciferin, which interact with oxygen, adenosine triphosphate (ATP), and calcium to produce light. That's what makes fireflies glow.*

February 24

I sketch diagrams in my drawing book the entire day. Only take bathroom breaks, chomp almonds and bananas. For two days, I skip breakfast and lunch but manage to drag myself to dinner where I wolf down the jollof rice, chickpeas, peppers, and mushrooms.

Lotem is thrilled that I'm beginning to engage my imagination; those are her words.

The Salvagers have started transporting people out of the underground shelters. I hope my mother is one of them.

February 25

I recall studying my father's schematics on the board in his basement study. Blueprints slowly form in my head.

February 27
I wake up during lunchtime, my head pounding. I feel a little feverish, so I stay in bed.

Taiye drops by with a tray of toast, omelettes, and oats. She sees the drawings scattered on the floor and says, "Whoa! Super cool."

February 28
I race down the hallway to the Guides' Suites and knock on Lotem's door.

"The fireflies," I exclaim the moment she opens the door.

"Slow down," she says, yawning.

"I think I have an idea, but I'm still not sure about it."

Lotem leans her head against the doorpost. "Can't it wait until morning?"

"It is morning technically."

Lotem slumps her shoulders. "Your idea had better be good, Gozzy." She motions me to a grey sofa. "Something to drink?" she asks.

A few hours later, Lotem creases her brow at the sheets of drawings in front of her and then says, "Explain it again."

I sip my creamy hot chocolate, savouring its sweetness. "They are diagrams of biosynthesis of Luciferin, Luciferase extraction processes, and a gradient method of how to convert chemical energy into light energy." I rub my thighs. "I know it sounds crazy, but what if we make a photovoltaic converter that absorbs cold light?"

Lotem sips her mug of mint tea. "What are you trying to say?"

I stutter with excitement. "If we redesign a reactor to catalyze substrates and create fissions high enough, we could generate electricity."

"You are losing me with all your ifs."

"When I was ten, my friends and I made lightning bug lanterns by catching fireflies and putting them in a glass jar with bits of grass, twigs, and leaves. And when there was a power cut, we brought out the jars and watched the glow. It was a wonder to look at."

"I'm sure the fireflies didn't find it wonderful."

"I have been diagramming how we can use an enzyme-assisted extraction method on fireflies."

Lotem widens her eyes. "Are you saying that we might be able to produce cold light just like fireflies do?"

"Yes. Bright lights with a very low voltage."

"That's brilliant. It sounds crazy, but this could work as long as we don't harm the fireflies."

I start to bite my nails. "There's also the possibility that it is a useless idea."

"I like the word possibility. As you know, the Commune is a space for possibility. And we try to translate ideas into action. Whether they work out or not, that's part of the process. Hope is action. That's all we can do. I'm so proud of you, Gozzy."

"Thank you so much, Lotem. But the challenge will be how to scale it up if we succeed in producing the prototype cold light."

"I wouldn't worry about that for now. Let's hear what the Guides say about your idea. In the meantime, the Salvagers will be here later in the day." Lotem kneads her brow thoughtfully. "I don't know if your mother will be among the survivors they are transporting, but I want you to know I am always here for you. I promise."

We have been sitting on her couch. Now I stand, gulp down my chocolate drink, and gaze at the green fields outside her windows.

• • •

Uchechukwu Peter Umezurike is an assistant professor of English at the University of Calgary. An alumnus of the International Writing Program (USA), Umezurike is a co-editor of Wreaths for Wayfarers, *an anthology of poems. He is the author of* Wish Maker *(Masobe Books, 2021),* Double Wahala, Double Trouble *(Griots Lounge Publishing, 2021) and* there's more *(University of Alberta Press, 2023).*

Facets of Transition, Eveline Kolijn. Etching.

FACETS OF TRANSITION/TRANSITION PRISM
Etching on BFK Rives paper, 2023,
48.3 x 33 cm or constructed, 14 x 14 x14 cm.
Download the Energy Futures dodecahedron to construct your own
Transition Prism.

Eveline Kolijn

STATEMENT

We have become accustomed to fossil fuels with a high concentration
of carbon and energy flowing through centralized refining and pow-
er-generating hubs, which are distributing energy to the consumer.
Low-emission, renewable energy sources have a more diffuse nature
and much lower potential energy. They function best in a decentralized system with various modes of local energy generation, and production in small units near the consumer. Energy can come from
solar, wind, geothermal heat, water, hydrogen, or any technology we
may still develop. Decarbonized fossil fuels and nuclear energy may
still be used in limited amounts, but they won't drive the system.
This multifaceted model must be managed by smart AI systems that
gauge consumption, production, and storage to shunt the energy
within this network in time from producers to consumers. When we
learn to operate this decentralized and decarbonized paradigm with
proper environmental controls, reduction of wasteful behaviour and
a more holistic and imaginative worldview, we can move towards a
multifaceted society that is sustainable and equitable.

• • •

Eveline Kolijn resides in Calgary. Eveline received a MA from Leiden University
in the Netherlands and a BFA from the Alberta University of the Arts. She
has participated in national and international exhibitions, residencies, and
public art projects. She has been published in scientific publications. She is
an Ambassador of the Energy Futures Lab. In 2019, she received the AUArts
Alumni Legacy Award.

Dependence/Grid (New Relic), Alex R. M. Thompson.
Etching and Aquatint.
Artist's statement is at the end of this chapter.

CHAPTER SEVENTEEN

A FOOT EACH IN TWO CANOES

Michael J. Leeb, Author
Alex R.M. Thompson, Artist

A FOOT EACH IN TWO CANOES

I.

Comment ça va ¿
Surely better than next year!
a response that seemingly implies
an impending ecological disaster
or perhaps worse ¿
the implication of *carbon capitalism*
an economic system of core and periphery
the core = (urban elites of politics, finance, and business) +
the periphery = (remote and marginalized northern Indigenous villages)
these peripheries as the geographical and cultural regions of the world
that have been ignored by
a deeply Eurocentric political culture
and socio-economic system
with evident vulnerabilities
entrenched wealth disparities
and structural inequalities
the peripheral hinterland

lacking in infrastructure and development
a core-periphery dichotomy
like a distorted echo chamber
asymmetrical
and emanating from the core
inherent within a malformed socio-political system
that reverberates aspirational echoes seeking autonomy
the message from the core replies with a predicated response
from a system of supply and demand
and an amorphous *invisible hand*
that benefits most   the *uber-rich*
structural realities necessitate
a fundamental shift towards equality
the imperative of nation-to-nation relations
and a departure from "ideological colonialism"
a colonialist methodology and a structure of economics
based upon capitalism   the accumulation and distribution of wealth
the world needs witness:
the preferential option for the poor
for: *The Lord hears the cry of the poor*
and their *righteous indignation*

II.
Comment ça va ¿
Keeping
despite the periphery being
disproportionately affected and vulnerable
marginalized and often forgotten
and most adverse to climate change
the reality of "off-grid" Indigenous communities of the North
those that live the problems

Technology proposes solutions
for these remote northern villages
the possibility of
microgrids for renewable energy
such as hydrogen or small modular reactors (wind and solar more probable)
as viable alternatives
although not yet fully developed
but rather as aspirational pilot projects
requiring additional research and feasibility studies
to be implemented at a future timeline

Though, do these Indigenous villages really desire such infrastructure ¿
Diesel fuel is considered a reliable source of fuel in cold weather climate
(of the 190 predominantly Indigenous northern villages in Canada are
"heavily dependent" on diesel)
yet in the south thought as
a stop-gap transitory measure
towards alternative energy

anecdotally one imagines that:
we want more energy efficient housing
energy affordability in the form of retrofits
such as high-efficiency wood stoves
and who pays for these alternatives anyway ¿

There is little appetite for unproven technologies
Cultural barriers considered
both problematic and justifiable reluctance
energy sovereignty of Indigenous communities
should "remain" (¿) "be"   sovereign
and collaboration essential
with informed prior consent
for a just transition

III.

A contradiction: technology will always save the day   .

really ¿ the skeptic replies

in a finite system of limited resources ¿

after-all   the world is a closed system that tends towards entropy

technology inevitably creates its' own problems

like a foot each in two canoes

or two row wampum

two parallel stories   yet   separate distinct coincidental

the story of "ideological colonialism"

 of Indigeneity and settler

beaded together have become one

a shared journey

inherent in its' finiteness

despite a vast geography

IV.

The world needs witness

a dedication to life at the margins

a re-emphasis from individual self-determination

towards a collective integral sustainability of

an ecological solidarity that supersedes

the world system order

a renewed support for social movements

that discern world problems

and promotes individuality as   minimalist responsible

consumption

Indigenous self-governance and economic autonomy

expressed in subsistence   hunting and fishing or the gathering

of wood fuel

as a cultural activity and

a restoration of wholeness

achieved through a dialogue exemplified

nation-to-nation equanimity
a universal solidarity of the common good

the world needs witness

V.

The Alberta Hydrogen Roadmap
seemingly has potential
as a path forward   toward net zero emissions
"blue" hydrogen fuel   light   storable   and energy-dense
producing limited emissions of carbon or greenhouse gases
thereby still necessitating carbon capture
Alberta already as a leading global producer

Although   "let's be clear"   this is not "green" hydrogen
produced from green forms of renewable energy
through a process of electrolysis
an energy initiative that surely benefits the energy security of the core
but does it have relevancy for the periphery ¿
could this energy initiative be considered
integral solidarity and sustainability ¿
of benefit to the marginalized far North
that too   has a fundamental right to development
requires: cultural and environmentally sensitive site-specific
compatibility
the implementation of small-scale microgrids
and fast charging EV stations
an expensive infrastructure installation
lacking economies of scale investment
in the remote proximate north

And what of announcements to develop mining in the North ¿
the intention to dramatically increase domestic production
and self-sufficiency of capacity
of minerals and rare earth metals

copper. nickel. lithium. cobalt. graphite
vanadium. tellurium. gallium. scandium.
magnesium. zinc. titanium. uranium.

ostensibly to bolster   the EV industry through the manufacture of
batteries
a mining ecosystem of federal tax credits to augment infrastructure
and industry
for the global EV supply of the core
with inherent consequences for lands and waters of the Northern
periphery
Burtynsky-esque images of dystopian landscapes
deeply inflicted with wounds of desolation
adverse effects for subsistence hunting and fishing   (as responsible
consumption)
the misappropriation of the rights of the others
concerns   as yet to be fully manifested
solidarity with reconciliation   as yet to be fully demonstrated
through economic development that asserts   due diligence and
cultural sensitivity

the reconciliation of wealth and cultural inequities
between the core and periphery
moral suasion towards
the fulfillment of integral human development
a moral imperative cries out! *to will the good of the other*   is true
solidarity

Notes on the poem

The salutations that begin the two first poem sequences are those of people living in the global south as described by Cardinal Michael Czerny, SJ in a web conference The Contribution of Catholicism for Sustainable Development sponsored by the Norman Patterson School of International Affairs, Carleton University; and The University of St. Michael's College, University of Toronto. April 26, 2022. The phrase "the world needs witness" is also attributed to Cardinal Czerny.

The term of "ideological colonialism" and "righteous indignation" were terms of speech used by Pope Francis in his Apology made to the Indigenous Delegation from Canada, on April 1, 2022 at the Vatican (Rome).

The phrases: "a foot each in two canoes", and "two row wampum" are used by the Six Nations Confederacy to refer to the history of colonialism in Canada.

The phrase: "a dedication to life on the margins" was expressed by Dr. Séverine Deneulin, (Oxford University)

during the web conference noted above.

The "anecdotes" in sequence II are based upon the research of Dr. Nick Mercer at Dalhousie University, from a webinar entitled: Advancing Energy Autonomy through Community-Based Research. March 29, 2022.

This research was conducted in Indigenous communities on the eastern shore of Labrador. I have extrapolated Dr. Mercer's research on Labrador to include the sentiment that is probable for most Indigenous villages in Canada.

Information in sequence V. is taken from articles in the *Globe and Mail*: "Kenney advances hydrogen-energy push." Emma Graney November 6, 2021. and

"Canadian miners back budget's plan for critical minerals." Ernest Scheyder & Steve Scherer. April 9, 2022.

The Greek word agape that translates as "love"; is defined as "to will the good of the other."

ELDERS WITH THE SUN

The buffalo
our Elder brother and sister
a gift of the Sun
pushed to extinction
returned to the Sun
as a conduit to the universe

The buffalo have returned again now
an intermediary of the Creator
to run with the rising and setting of the Sun
always in the direction of the Sun
the first solar powered battery
harnessing the energy of the Sun
restoring the vibrancy of native prairie grasslands
that sequester carbon even more efficiently
than boreal forests
when there are problems   remember
go to the buffalo
learn from the Elder with the Sun

Notes on the poem

The italicized verses of this poem are from comments made by
Diandra Bruised Head (Kainai)
That were expressed during an Energy Futures Lab Zoom meeting on
May 26, 2022.

• • •

Michael J. Leeb is a Chippewa Cree/German visual artist, poet, writer, and historian. Michael was a regular contributor to OnSite Review *and has been published in* The Nashwaak Review; Existere; Red Ink; Lemon Theory; Barzakh; Grain; *and* The Canadian Journal of Native Studies. *Michael was the Writer-in-Residence at the Gushul Writer's Cottage in 2013, and received a project grant in 2014 from the Canada Council for the Arts for a poetry project that resulted in the publication of a book of poetry entitled:* Spirit of Place: Earth, Wind, Sky, Water; *published in 2016 by SkyDancer Books (an imprint of Eschia Books). Michael was a finalist for the Eliza So Fellowship in 2019.*

DEPENDENCE GRID (NEW RELIC)
Etching, aquatint, spit bite, scraper on Hahnemühle
Copperplate, 33 x 48.3cm, 2022

Alex R.M. Thompson

STATEMENT

Dependence/Grid (New Relic) reflects on the deeply entwined and long-established relationship between coal and energy generation in this province. While carbon emissions targets must be ambitious in the face of catastrophic climate change, the legacy of fossil fuels underlies the structure of the power grid. The conversation surrounding coal extraction is broad, including questions of habitat destruction, embodied emissions in resources yet to be burned, and relationships between Indigenous communities, the land, mining corporations, and economic interests. The complex web of considerations and consequences begins to resolve into an abstract grid in the printed work, its form carved onto the underlying portrait of extraction activities that irrevocably scar and alter the landscape. As it stands, nearly 36 percent of Alberta's electricity is produced from coal sources, and the province "boasts" the largest coal fleet in the country. Ontario has already entirely phased coal out of its energy grid, and gradually Alberta aims to do the same. Staring into the gaping pit of resource extraction, collectively we must aspire to make the shift rapidly.

• • •

Alex R.M. Thompson is a printmaker/artist currently based in Edmonton, Alberta. His work engages with the built environment, reflecting on the timeliness/timelessness of architecture, how structures shape the individuals occupying them, and the compression of distances that technology enables. Thompson holds a BFA from OCAD University in Toronto, and an MFA from the University of Alberta.

Water Tender (detail), Liz Ingram.
Inkjet and drypoint on Hahnemühle cotton rag paper.
Artist's statement is at the end of this chapter.

CHAPTER EIGHTEEN

OUR FUTURE IS WATER

Mar'ce Merrell, Author
Liz Ingram, Artist

KIND FRIENDS, gather at the river. Here, where the Bow River flows from the eastern slopes of the Rocky Mountains and through a man-made reservoir and dam, Ghost Lake.

Settle into a rock seat under the full moon in November, named after the beaver. An ecosystem engineer with the motivation of a survivalist, the beaver will take advantage of the light to winterize their lodge.

We bundle in layers of fleece and down. We warm our hands and bellies with mugs of hot chocolate. On this spectacular night, the earth's shadow will shroud the moon and through the darkness, we will observe a reddish sphere of light. We will perceive differently. Imagine with more urgency. Like the beaver, we will let our experience guide us.

From the river shore, we hear water sounds: the swish of a whorl behind a rock, burbles from the shallows, and a near-silent hum from the channel. The sound of water. The sound of energy.

We begin to think back and back to moments at the river's edge, or a childhood creek, a frozen lake, a day at the ocean, the time we danced in the rain, marvelled at the hail, or caught snowflakes on our tongues. Our lives, we may remember, are bound with water. We don't often think about it, but we know we each of us began life in the water-wombs of our mothers. How often do we feel our reliance on water?

How often are we thirsty?

Sitting here in our winter clothes, waiting for a cosmic event to wow us, do any of us think of the story of water? Do we remember how our earliest ancestors had to live near a freshwater source and collect rain to survive longer than three days? Many of us continue to be water carriers, walking water from the source to our families, miles each day.

How many of us know the weight of water?

Sitting under the full moon shadow of the dam, do any of us remember how the first dams changed everything? With electric power, manufacturing expanded. Wires enabled us to create electric grids and our energy could be transported. All energy creation relies on water.

We use more water for electricity production than we drink.

We hear river sounds, but we don't hear the water moving through our bodies. We drink from our mugs, but we don't wonder if the water is safe.

Have we forgotten how important water is?

We gather at the river tonight, thirsty to watch the moon turn a deep red in the shadow of the earth. We are here to look into the darkness. Together.

• • •

Every gathering begins a story.

This story comes from all of us, all of us who gather on this night of rare happenings, the third full lunar eclipse in twelve months. We're here to listen and to create a new story from the gathering of all the stories.

A businessman begins, "Canada is not a water-secure country, even though we rank in the top 10 globally for annual renewable resources per capita."

Some of us sigh, why does every gathering end up so...political... endangered?

A scientist says, "The future of energy is the future of water. All sources of energy require water. Extracting raw materials needs water. Any thermal process needs to be cooled, with water. Biofuels can't grow without water. We can't power turbines without water. Transporting water to our homes and to our fields uses water. Even making water safe to drink, uses water!"

A hedgefund investment strategist nods, "Water has value."

Some of us sigh, so much depends on the actions we take, so much is at stake.

For a long time, no one else speaks. No one reaches for their cellphone. We listen to our thoughts making sense of the words. We feel our resistance or acceptance of the statements offered.

No one googles, is the future of energy, the future of water? Or, what to do when you can't sit still and you need to.

We can feel how our thirst for energy is tied to our survival. We shift uneasily in our seats, but we stay. We continue to listen.

A father speaks, "Floods, drought, fires and toxic algae blooms threaten our future. From 2000-2017 the cost of trying to make peace with our water troubles (and we haven't made peace) was $28 billion."

We sit. We think. Obsessively, we think. What are the margins of error in a calculation of a number like $28 billion? How many people have to boil their water in order to drink it? How many people have to drink water shipped in by truck?

A teacher speaks, "Our water resources are being poisoned by resource extraction, processing and transportation of oil and gas, ore, and pulp and paper. Intensive agriculture for crop and livestock production threatens the health of our eco-systems."

Our thoughts spin. Our muscles contract. Our jaws tense. What about our jobs, our families' livelihood, all we've worked hard for, our property values? Are we doomed to re-create the world we know?

From downstream, we hear The Beaver slap its tail.

A hydrologist speaks, "Canada is warming at two times the global average. Climate change is shifting our hydrological cycle. We predict decreases in agriculture production and hydropower generation. We predict increases in flood and drought."

Our thoughts scream at some of us, What is a hydrological cycle? Predictions? Only in the worst-case scenario.

A young voice speaks, "Guys, guys, listen! Don't we need lakes and rivers to be healthy so we can have healthy plants and animals and forests? What if we can't play in the water? Do you think video games are enough for me? Is that what you've all been working for? So I can build in Minecraft? So I can race Mario and Luigi? Why don't you care about water enough to protect it? Why don't you care enough about me?"

Some of us think, Why is there a kid here? Trying to manipulate all of us into– "Doing the right thing"? The right thing is too complicated for a kid to understand. I am so bored. I wish I'd brought beer. Whose idea was this?

Some of us remember fishing as a child, floating down a river, swimming in the ocean. I love water. But, what can I do? We're so far away from being able to solve...anything.

"Our communication is a problem," a lawyer says, "The jurisdictional fragmentation, fighting over territory, and overall inequity of our systems... generating and implementing a common water management vision needs cooperation. Our separation is harmful."

An immigrant speaks, "We watched the Aral Sea disappear. The fourth largest lake in the world. Gone. Irrigated to death. Now, we get sandstorms. And pesticide dust flies for hundreds of kilometres. Air poisoning."

"There are more than a trillion litres of toxic oilsands waste stored in tailings ponds near Alberta's Athabasca River," a journalist shakes their head, " — and they're leaking."

"My memory of water is having to cross it. I...," a mother's voice trails off.

Another mother says, "Drink water, I told my kids. Not pop. People forgot about the guy who mined arsenic, 127 tonnes in a year, and sent it off to Nova Scotia. My whole community, back in Newfoundland? Cancer everywhere."

Some of us feel very sleepy. Our eyelids feel heavy. Some of us feel nauseous. We rub our bellies.

Some of us think, We need water. We need clean and healthy water and healthy plants and animals. There must be a way. There must be a way.

A young adult speaks, "We are slowly committing suicide."

We've lost some of us now. A few are slumped over. Dreaming about a future vacation on a cruise ship, building a bunker, starting a brewery, going back home to Saskatchewan and helping with the harvest.

Dreaming of ancestors in chains in a ship hold, of stomach cramps and nausea, of surfing and sailing and free diving, of being tucked into bed and kissed goodnight by their moms and dads, descending into the waves of sleep.

Here under the light of the full moon, on a night when so much is possible, a warrior is about to speak. She calls herself a Warrior for the Human Spirit.

Her 23 and me reports says she's mostly northern European, Irish and British, and she's got some Viking in her. She's .3 percent Indigenous. She has no nation, no cultural experience. She was baptized and raised Catholic. She has Hindu, Christian, Muslim, Buddhist, Indigenous friends. She reads a lot. Listens to podcasts. She is a mix of all the experiences she has had, all the places she's lived, and all the voices she's heard. She's fought inner battles all her life with what to believe, what to hope for, and how to live. And, tonight, her voice rises from the gathering.

"We cannot nap. We all need to listen."

Remember, this is a night we agree to gather. We gather to be wowed, to see how, in an instant, for the third time in twelve months, the moon will fall in the earth's shadow. In the earth's shadow, the moon will change colour and our perspective of her will shift. We will see her differently.

Whenever we see differently, we open to the possibility of change. We open to the possibility of creating a new story.

We listen to the Warrior for the Human Spirit:

I have a water story. About how I got to know water. About how I got to know myself. About why I'm here, among all of us.

It's a painful story. You don't end up as a warrior without war stories.

In January 2016, I could no longer live in my lodge of safety
and denial. I'd run out of resources. My health was going downhill
and the job I loved made me cry, many times a day. I didn't show
up for people I loved. I trusted people I shouldn't have. It was hard
to remember my problems were not other people's fault.

I noticed a cycling of past trauma: the freaking out, sleeping
but never resting, weeks of constant movement and distractions.
I kept a stash of heavy-duty painkillers in case I couldn't live with
myself any longer.

One day I looked in the mirror and thought, I hate you.

I was starting to look like Philomena, a woman I knew years
ago. I remembered her eyes, worn-out and sad. We were at a
party, each of us drinking from red wine glasses big enough for a
goldfish to live in.

"I mostly hate myself," she said. Her eyes were cloudy.

I stared into my wine glass, nodded my head, and walked
away. I remember thinking, "She has to be able to do something,
She's got kids."

Months later the light in her eyes was different. Outward
Bound, the Women of Courage program, she said, taught her how
strong she was. I never forget her story.

Outward Bound.

I wandered around my basement suite, irritated by my landla-
dy's vacuuming above me, and tried to imagine my future. Here.
Anywhere. Nothing came. I took a bath to wash away, cry away,
the sadness. I looked in the mirror again.

You have to save yourself. Your children need you. Your
grandchildren.

I googled Outward Bound. They were accepting applications
for the Woman of Courage program for two more days.

In 2016, I owned a fridge magnet: I Love Not Camping. I
brought it from the family home we sold when we separated. I
didn't want to forget about my previous 5-star life.

For weeks after I applied, my stomach churned when I thought
about Outward Bound. What if they accepted me? What if they

didn't? I'd already told them about the violence from my past, the echo I was experiencing in my current relationships. They needed to interview my therapist, they needed to consider the needs and skills of the group (7 women and 2 eco-therapists). They needed to understand my emotional stability.

To keep myself from drowning in the shame I felt about my past and my present and my fear of the future, I lived my life like I could divide it, separate it. Lots of people live like that. You can dam a river. You can divide a life. You create one channel for work, another for family, another one for the past, one for happy you, one for sad you, one for you who wants friends. It works for a lot people. But some dams fill up with silt or the river dries up. In my case, all the dams were breached. I was the victim of a continuous inner flood.

Could I spend two weeks canoeing in the wilderness with two female guides/eco-therapists and a group of seven women who were as hurt and aspiring as me?

When Outward Bound called all I had to do was get myself to Vancouver Island, I almost told the coordinator I couldn't come. Mid-objection, she told me I was a good candidate.

I used her words to create a lodge inside myself, a warm future. Sometimes I dreamed of sleeping under the stars, sometimes drowning. My fear receded and spiked, like a tide. In late June, on the drive west, through the Rocky Mountains, I stopped my car by the side of the road. I walked into the forest thinking I wouldn't be coming back out. I didn't want to face the whole me, the pain I'd suffered, the harm I'd caused. No way could I overcome it all. In the forest I heard other voices, though.

Your children depend on you. Your grandchildren need you.

Desolation Sound is an ocean passage between Vancouver Island and the mainland. It's big, wide water. Lots of people kayak close to the shores of islands. Canoeing, though, is uncommon. Dangerous. Water in a canoe swamps it. And canoeing requires communication to respond to changes in the water. None of us were very experienced. Our guides navigated us in the right direction, but our resources, physical and emotional, mattered. I felt the weight of responsibility for my canoe mates. I also learned I could trust them.

Surviving on salt water is a challenge. You need fresh water. Our canoes doubled as water-heavy shipping vessels with all the litres of water we carried. We paddled short, hard days. We paddled big, rolling waves, rising and falling, like massive breaths, like whales breaching. Shipping vessels and luxury yachts left wakes of fast-moving cross-current waves. My hands ached from gripping my paddle. My jaw clicked with tension every time I opened my mouth. We weren't safe next to land, either. Water churned in the competing currents, spilled over the bow, pooled at my feet.

From the back of the canoe, I cried, laughed, and freaked out, but no one seemed bothered by my fear. We were immersed in beauty: the water, the sky, the land. We all had fears. I never admitted I was afraid of drowning. I'd nearly drowned several times in my life. I didn't tell anyone about my recurring night-mares. I refused to swim, though, even with a lifejacket.

Tides change in 7-hour shifts in Desolation Sound. The water level against the land might be one metre high or over five metres high. We hauled our tents, food, water, and canoes sometimes 10 metres straight up to the protection of flat-ish land. We slept on weather-beaten rocks. We watched the sun rise and set every day. I experienced vivid memories and dreams of ways I lived my life, eyes-wide-open-but-asleep, a zombie in disguise.

The main event of the Outward Bound Women of Courage program is the solo night. All the paddling, the friendship, the sharing, the laughter, the skill building leads up to a night where each woman sleeps with only a sleeping pad and a sleep-ing bag, far away from one another, from the guides. Solo night is twenty-four hours to meet yourself: whoever you are, wher-ever you're from, whatever context you're in. I wasn't sure I could do it, but I wanted to.

In addition to our sleeping gear, we carried dry food in a plastic bag, a litre of water, an envelope, a few pieces of writing paper, and a pen. At low tide, I crossed a rock garden from one island to another. On the second island, I found a south-west facing ledge just wide enough for me and my sleeping bag with a view of the water and under an all-afternoon sunbeam-fall.

We had a task to accomplish with the writing paper and the envelope: Write a letter to yourself. Fold it. Seal it in the envelope. Address it to yourself. You'll receive it six months from now. I had writer's block. I wanted the letter to change my life, but I had no imagination for the future beyond my want for a different way to live.

I picked my way through steep rocks down to the ocean. I let my toes drop in. Purple starfish clung to the rocks underneath me. Birds flew in a big swoop. An arbutus tree stretched, impossibly, over the water. The peeling bark on the tree reminded me of snakes shedding their skin. I waited for something more than a metaphor to inspire me. Nothing came. I ate almost all my food by 2 p.m. I was wasting my 24 hours of courage.

My belly full of pepperoni sticks, nuts and dried fruit, I laid down on my narrow ledge to digest. I fell asleep. I'll never forget waking up. I jolted awake, slipped, careened four or five feet down the rocky hillside. My right foot screamed in pain.

I pulled a bee stinger from my big toe on my right foot. It was already starting to swell. It really hurt. I wasn't allergic to bees, but I wanted to be. I wanted to have a good reason to call my solo night quits. What was the point if I couldn't write a letter to myself? I'd learned enough, hadn't I? It didn't have to be perfect, did it?

I sat on my ledge and looked out. The sun, low in the sky, created sparks and sparkles of light on the water. Dancing light. I noticed my head tilted to the right. As if I were curious. Listening.

I found my journal where I stashed it, in the bottom of my sleeping bag. If I couldn't write myself a letter, I could at least write something in my journal.

I dreamed new dreams of waking up in a different place with

different music. The sounds were more percussive, and bird song. Like the sound of a canoe paddle and the sound of water and the sound of birds.

There will be a day when being outside, free, is so easy for you—that you are able to go without question. You are unfettered.

And the community you needed, the family? You created them—you brought them into the world and nurtured them and they are part of your every day now.

There will be a day when you aren't afraid to tell the truth of who you are. You're not afraid to be yourself. One day, in fact, your self moves to the side because other selves interest you.

I found those words a few weeks ago.

I'm here because what I wrote my future self came true. I learned to listen to myself and to imagine a healthy future. I became a canoeist and I show up for my family.

I found a way to love myself, despite all my problems.

I found a way to love water, despite my fear of her near-death.

I want to save them both.

All of us are awake. We're all sitting on our rock chairs. We're warm. We're quiet. We've cried. We've laughed. We are about to be wowed.

The full moon light has been fading for a while now and a reddish hue has been increasing in intensity. Quiet, we witness the last of the moonlight disappear. We ooh and ahh at the red glow of the moon in the earth's shadow—a moon still there, but seen so differently now. Under the glow of the red moon, we listen.

A mother speaks, "So, what I'm hearing is all of us need to go on an Outward Bound Women of Courage program?"

The Warrior smiles, "An experience like Outward Bound is a strategy for meeting yourself. Meeting yourself is the beginning. It happens in stillness. Quiet. Find quiet, stay in quiet."

"We were in denial and then they didn't listen to us," an immigrant shakes her head. "Better to face the truth as soon as you know it."

"We have an opportunity," a businessman taps his foot against the rocks.

"We know water has value," a hedgefund investment strategist says, "Perhaps we need to use a different metric?"

"It's so beautiful. This sky, this earth, the water. I can feel this beauty," a mother wipes tears from her eyes. "All women are carriers of the water."

"Let's remember," a hydrologist offers, "Given the right business model, access to support, and resources, the Canadian water sector can deliver water technology, management, capacity, and predictive tools to emerging markets, particularly in developing countries, to accelerate greatly needed sustainable water resources management."

"We can change our systems," a lawyer clears his throat, "In Two-Eyed Seeing people come together to view the world through an Indigenous lens with one perspective, one eye, while the other eye sees through a Western lens."

"Water needs us," the youngest voice adds. "We need water."

"We start with a hypothesis," says a scientist. "A framing of a question. Perhaps we need to be asking different questions, more questions, more often."

"The government is us." A grandmother stands. "We need action."

A poet stands. "Coherence of vision requires relationship."

"In the face of great adversity." A father stands. "The courageous take a step forward."

"We granted personhood to the Magpie River in Quebec." A teacher stands. "Out of respect for water, many nations do not sell water. It is a being."

"How can we love something we don't know?" A young adult's voice begs us to listen. "How can we save something we don't love? What happens if we don't love ourselves? Or each other?"

"Water needs us! Water needs us!" The youngest voice chants. "Water needs us!"

We feel our hearts expand and contract. Love and fear. We allow both. We listen to each other's voices, again and again, under the red moon. In the early hours of the next day, we walk, side-by-side up the hill and past the dam.

One of us began to write a new story:

We gathered the night of the Beaver Full Moon. On this spectacular night, in the darkness lit by a reddish moon, we perceived differently and imagined with more urgency. Like the beaver, we let our experience guide us.

Our future is water.

The future of food and shelter, of electricity, of energy for economic development, is water.

Our future is water.

. . .

Mar'ce Merrell is a writer. She is also a canoeist. Neither beginner nor expert, she survives long trips in the wilderness. She relies on her paddling partner when she's distracted by falling in love with the outside world. She jumped into Ghost Lake on Thanksgiving Day and swam to the shore. Her son challenged the whole family. Everyone agreed.

Water Tender, Liz Ingram.
Inkjet and drypoint on Hahnemühle cotton rag paper.

WATER TENDER
Inkjet and drypoint on Hahnemühle cotton rag paper,
2022, 33x 48.3 cm

Liz Ingram

STATEMENT

At an early age growing up in India, I was exposed to extremes of physical deprivation butted up against heightened sensuality, rich colours, sounds, smells and ritual practices. I believe that these early experiences predisposed me to my continuing investigations of the human condition with a focus on the human body in nature. For over 40 years most source material has been garnered from a particular place/lake/stream in the northern boreal forest of Alberta. Using printed images, paper, ink, glass, light, shimmering pixels, and fabric, I strive to give the viewer an experience that will generate a sense of care and love for our environment. My work is an attempt to express more fully a 'truth' about the pressing need to love the totality of the 'natural' world, to arouse the sense that loving water, loving earth, moss, fungi, fauna—loving our environ-ment—is to love and sustain humanity.

• • •

Liz Ingram was born in Argentina in 1949 and grew up in Delhi, Mumbai and Toronto. She is a Distinguished Professor Emerita at, the University of Alberta. Honours include Order of Canada; U. of A. Distinguished Alumni Award; Edmonton Hall of Fame; RSC; RCA. She has exhibited in over 300 exhibitions in North and South America, Europe, the Middle East and the Far East.

Narcissus Reimagined, Tara Manyfingers.
Etching on dyed Japanese paper.
Artist's statement is at the end of this chapter.

CHAPTER NINETEEN

HOW CAN THE FUTURE GO REALLY, REALLY WELL?

Maggie Hanna, Author
Tara Manyfingers, Artist

Energy transition is the moonshot of our generation.
Nature has evolved an entire planet full of regenerative animal/
plant/fungi/bacterial systems across the many life-giving water and
land regions across the world, each one adapted to the local circumstances and weather patterns. Nothing is wasted. My Cree sister,
Moss, refers to all the animals and plants and rivers and mountains
as All Our Relations; We are all 'us' together; There is no 'other'."
Modern ways of living modify land to feed our increasing numbers,
leaving less and less of what 'All Our Relations' need to live. This
cannot go on for long. We live because everything else does.

Hydrocarbon energy (coal, oil, and natural gas) is given to us by
the earth and is an amazing set of molecules, comprised of hydrogen
and carbon, hence the name. Over 80 percent of our current global
energy comes from burning hydrocarbons. They are affordable,
energy-dense, store energy for seasons to years, easy to transport,
and reliable.

We have built ingenious hydrocarbon infrastructure systems
which provide home heating, water purification and distribution,
sewage systems, fueling stations for transport, and fuel for agriculture machinery to feed ourselves ... to name but a few. Our lifespan
and quality of life have increased over the past 200+ years because

of hydrocarbons. We have burnt hydrocarbons for energy, emitting large amounts of heat, carbon dioxide (CO_2) and water vapour (H_2O), into the atmosphere for a couple of centuries. Water vapour and CO_2 are powerful greenhouse gases; however, H_2O remains in the atmosphere for only a few days to a couple of weeks, whereas CO_2 hangs around in the order of decades to centuries.

There are unintended consequences to burning hydrocarbons. We have been so busy wondering "Can we do it?" that we didn't stop to ask "Should we do it?" The lion's share of human-caused greenhouse gases comes from burning hydrocarbons—around 62 percent. In 2022, CO_2 measurements varied between 414-422ppm (parts per million) in our atmosphere. That is a lot. The average CO_2 concentration over the past 400,000 years has been 200-280 ppm. I was born at 315 ppm. We have run out of safe room in the atmosphere for more CO_2. We have reached a planetary boundary.

Climate change is upon us. It is changing the nature of Nature ... the local circumstances, and weather patterns that we, and all our relations, have become adapted to and are dependent upon. Climate change effects take the form of probabilities. There have always been extreme weather events, however, these days more extreme weather is more likely to occur.

One of our biggest assumptions is that the climate emergency is an issue. It's not ... it's an era.

How does climate change work anyway?

Our planet has a natural blanket of heat-trapping gases in the atmosphere, which is dominantly CO_2. This natural blanket keeps the Earth about 30 degrees Celsius warmer than it would be otherwise. When sunlight shines through the atmosphere like a window... and hits the Earth, it changes from light to heat. The heat is reflected back up into space, but on the way, some heat gets trapped in the atmosphere by heat-trapping gases, dominantly CO_2, just like a blanket trapping body heat on a cold night.

Canadian climate scientist Dr. Katharine Hayhoe explains our problem very well. By digging up and burning oil, gas and coal, which releases large quantities of CO_2, we are wrapping an *extra* blanket of heat-trapping gases around the planet. If your grandma snuck in at night and put an extra down comforter over you, you would wake up sweating. Similarly, our Earth is starting to run a fever because of this extra blanket we have wrapped around it. Climate change acts like a chronic fever in your body. If your body ran a 2-degree chronic fever of 39°C, you wouldn't operate very well either.

Why change our energy systems now?
Energy is the lynchpin, it is connected to *everything*. The United Nations have determined 17 Sustainable Development Goals which include things like:

- #1 No Poverty
- #2 Zero Hunger
- #6 Clean Water and Sanitation
- #8 Decent Work and Economic Growth
- #11 Sustainable Cities and Communities

All 17 goals depend on #7 ... Affordable and Clean Energy. We must work to decarbonize our energy systems now because much of the new infrastructure needed to stop and reverse climate change easily requires at least ten years to design, permit,and build. The longer we wait, the more damage is done to weather systems, Nature, and humanity. And the more it will cost.

How might we get our energy in 2050?
Any desirable future starts with a clear vision of how we want it to look... what we want and not just what we will settle for. Seneca said, "If one does not know to which port one is sailing, no wind is favourable." Gotta know where you are going.

The Energy Transition principles are:

- There is no such thing as "more sustainable." We are sustainable or we are not
- There is no such thing as 'clean' energy.... only energy sources with lower lifecycle Greenhouse Gas (GHG) emissions than others
- Maintain "Energy on Demand" and do not allow the system to devolve into "Energy Only as Available"
- Electrify everything we can
- Reduce and then stop burning liquid fossil fuels for transportation
- Reduce and then stop burning fossil fuels for industrial-scale heat systems that don't use carbon capture
- Reduce and then stop burning fossil fuels for building heat and water heat
- Convert main grid to multiple connected microgrid systems
- Increase energy storage of all kinds
- Stop energy waste... which is currently 30 percent
- There are two scales of emissions solutions: large-scale industrial emissions, and aggregated small-scale emissions like buildings and vehicles. Solutions for each scale are different
- Change personal behaviour

Below is my vision of the future decarbonized world energy mix by 2050. The point of this list is to see that there are many options. Every region's low-carbon energy system will look different based on its resource endowments, finances, needs, and social acceptance. Each technology is like a colour in the paint box. Every country or region will choose and mix its colours into their own amazing painting. We must ensure all countries have access to all colours they need.

- **Low Carbon Electricity** totaling 50-70 percent of world energy demand. Today we are at 22 percent. This means world grids must expand capacity by 2-3 times to charge Battery Electric Vehicles (BEV) and run electric heat pumps, which are the workhorses of the distributed portion of the energy transition.

- **Nuclear Plants** will power 35-45 percent of global grids. Today we are at 11 percent. Combined with grid expansion, we will need about 7-9 times more nuclear capacity than we have today. Focus on Small Modular Nuclear Reactors, molten salt cooling, and Thorium in fuel mixes.
- **Firm power** is power we can count on to be there when we call for it. Some examples are natural gas power plants with Carbon Capture, Utilization and Sequestration (CCUS), hydropower (including dams, run of river, pumped hydro), geothermal, and municipal waste to electricity. Tidal energy is semi-firm as it provides intermittent power at very regular intervals.
- **Intermittent Power** is power that cannot be counted upon when called for. Wind, solar, agrisolar (including growing food on the same land with sheep, vegetables and grains).
- **Hydrogen** totals 35-45 percent of world energy demand. It is made in many different ways and performs many different services.
- **Biomass** will be 4-8 percent of world energy demand including biofuels, plant wastes, garbage dumps, and poop. Nature in her wisdom uses waste biomass to build soils and keep the soil beastie-buggies healthy and thriving. We can not take too much.
- **Hydrocarbon burning** will be <15 percent of world energy demand. Today we are at over 80 percent.
  - **Coal** will be fully retired by 2050. Coal emissions are highest in CO_2 emissions and other health-damaging pollutants.
  - **Oil-based** liquid transport fuels retired. Seventy percent of every barrel of oil is used for transport fuels and will be replaced in the market.
    - For land transport, it will be replaced by batteries, Hydrogen, and methanol
    - For shipping, it will be replaced with methanol,

nuclear and some ammonia
- For flight, it will be replaced with batteries, Hydrogen and Sustainable Airline Fuel (SAF)
- Natural gas used sparingly for hard-to-abate industrial uses and with full CCUS
- **Petrochemicals** useful and therefore will be made from hydrocarbons in 2050.
- **Eliminate Energy Waste.** Currently 30 percent of total energy generated is wasted. If we stopped this, we would have enough energy to support the extra population by 2050 and lift a lot of people out of energy poverty.
- **Expand Atmospheric CO_2.** Capture as fast as we can. Inject captured CO_2 into deep geological formations, re-carbonize our soils, grow mixed forests for natural habitat, grow managed tree lots for timber used in the built environment, and use new technologies for making useful solid Carbon molecules out of CO_2.
- **Increase Energy Storage Capacity.** This is a partial list from longest to shortest duration storage... focus on the fact there are a lot of options:
  - Hydrogen (in salt caverns, in delivery pipelines, as metal hydrides, compressed Hydrogen, liquid Hydrogen, as methane, as ammonia, etc.)
  - Pumped hydro
  - Compressed air
  - Gravity storage
  - Hot rocks and sand
  - Batteries of all sorts
  - Flywheels
  - Supercapacitors... and others

The energy sources and principles detailed above are doable and provide reasonable ways to replace hydrocarbon burning in the world. The pathways are clear. We must come together, take thoughtful collective action, execute projects well, and fund them. We could rationalize our way out of designing and building the energy future we want because of the risk, the cost, and the unknown. Acting now will cost money... but not acting, or acting later will be many times more expensive, and more perilous in the long run. Climate change is an emergency. We are not treating it that way yet. When we treat something as an emergency, impossible things become possible.

Ralph Torrie, Research Director of Corporate Knights says, "We are up against climate change impacts that are increasingly unalterable. Five to seven percent of the entire economic activity of Canada will be devoted to floods, wildfires, and storm surges by the end of this decade." He says, "Canada has a $2,000 Billion/year economy, and spending $126 B/year every year for the next decade will bring us a long way towards meeting our decarbonization goals. And we can afford it."

It is important to understand that the goal of a Global Decarbonized Energy System by 2050 is different from the pathways we need to get there. A pathway starts from where you are... and takes you to where you want to go. One can't take a step from where one is not. This means we will be doing things in the early stages of the pathway that we won't be doing by 2050. Burning hydrocarbons and pooping the resulting CO_2 into the atmosphere is one of those things. We can't physically turn off all hydrocarbons today without a lot of suffering and death. We are not yet ready with a set of workable low-carbon alternatives that we, as citizens, can affordably choose. But we are getting there. The early phases of energy transition pathway will have to be accomplished on the back of hydrocarbons, because there is nothing else.

How do we phase out hydrocarbons?

Coal burning will be gone by 2050, and some replaced by very-low carbon natural gas burning (both fossil and biogas) with >90 percent CO_2 captured into solid carbons. This CO_2 capture technology needs an industrial scale to work (it does not work at small scales), so home heat and personal transportation will be electrified.

Oil is another matter. Seventy percent of every barrel of oil is used for liquid transport fuels: gasoline, diesel, jet, and bunker. We have all the technology we need *today* to eliminate our liquid fuel demand, and each of us has an important part to play in that. Here's how. You may have heard: "The dog wags the tail. The tail does not wag the dog." Oil companies exist to meet our demand. They are the tail and we consumers are the dog. They will keep producing products we want to buy. We can choose to stop buying gasoline and diesel, progressively shrinking the demand side of the oil market. The less we use, the less they make and the faster they will turn their engineering to low-carbon energy uses, like hydrogen production and transportation infrastructure. It is up to us, consumers, to make cleaner transportation fuel choices. The sooner the better. Burning gasoline and diesel will become more expensive over time. The carbon tax will accelerate that. It makes hydrocarbon use more expensive, which means consumers and industry will choose cheaper, cleaner options.

How messy might grids get this next decade?
An electrical grid only works well when it is balanced. That means whenever we take an electron out to run the coffee grinder, another electron is put into the grid, in real-time. Our world grids run dominantly on hydrocarbon fuels, with some hydro and a bit of nuclear, supplied by central power plants. Power has been affordable at a medium pricing level. Grid reliability came for free due to the firm nature of our power sources.

Today, we have very cheap solar and wind power, but they are intermittent so do not have grid reliability. We must design new systems with built-in reliability. We also need a variety of backup power options, all connected by digital controls in a smart grid to balance it all. When the grid is stressed, the backup power sources switch on. It will take at least a decade to install these backup technologies and integrate them into a workable system under digital smart grid control. Until then, we can anticipate more blackouts. The transition will likely be messy, but you can do things to be more robust.

What can you do?
You can participate in society and energy transition, by exercising your individual choices. Individuals and families can contribute to long-term changes by making informed, conscious choices. We can choose to be part of the solution. Start with intention. A person can do exactly the same thing with a different intent and get a different result. What is your intention? Think about it. Write it down. And then ask yourself what actions you want to take to manifest your intention in the world.

We have things we can control, and things over which we have influence. Individuals and families have control over choices that are within our finances, power, and creativity to accomplish. We can influence the system in which we find ourselves through active and repeated positive communication, with friends, family, neighbours, and politicians. Don't scare people with negative climate facts as it puts them into fright/flight/freeze where nothing gets done. Instead, tell people why climate change matters to you, and offer real things we can do together to mitigate it. That is empowering.

Exercise control over your home retrofit
Eighty percent of the current buildings will exist in 2050. Many require upgrading so less energy is needed to run them. We can choose to retrofit our homes to be energy efficient and emit less CO_2, by adding insulation, replacing leaky or old windows with triple panes, changing leaky doors, and adding a heat pump to use most of the time. Keep your natural gas furnace/boiler as a backup for when it gets too cold for the heat pump to work; below -28C. You can use this heat pump to cool your home in summer. You might install solar panels and/or a tiny wind turbine on your roof... and possibly a home battery system. In a blackout, you can power your own home and support your neighbours.

In Canada, there are government incentives to help finance this retrofit. Some jurisdictions have programs in place whereby the homeowner borrows all the retrofit money from the municipality. The payback is attached to the deed at a rate less than the extra energy savings and happens over decades.

Exercise control over your transportation

When buying a car, the first thing you can do is switch to a zero-emission vehicle (ZEV). Current options are Battery Electric Vehicle (BEV), Hydrogen Fuel Cell Electric Vehicle (HFCEV or just FCEV), a Plug-in-Hybrid, or a Hybrid. Taking the bus/train, and active transport like bicycling when feasible, are great options. My rule of thumb is... if you currently drive a gasoline vehicle, then 80 percent of the time you are better off going BEV. If you currently drive a diesel vehicle, then 90 percent of the time you are better off with an HFCEV... once there is sufficient Hydrogen fueling in your area. Why? An HFCEV costs significantly more to run but has some advantages: long distances, heavy loads, high-duty cycles, frequently towing equipment, cold weather and remote wilderness driving. Forward thinkers will likely choose BEV for the lower operational and maintenance costs, especially if they have access to home charging.

If you are not yet comfortable with a BEV, then the second-best choice is a Plug-In-Hybrid. I don't recommend a straight-up Hybrid because they charge the battery when running on gasoline. A plug-in hybrid has a much larger battery and can charge the battery from anywhere on the grid. Most daily city driving can be done on battery power with gasoline as a backup for remote driving. If you choose to buy an Internal Combustion Engine (ICE) (gasoline or diesel) anytime soon, rethink. It might last 10-15 years. Fossil fuel costs will progressively increase as carbon taxes increase. ICE machines will likely be banned from driving on some, if not most, roads before then. It might also become harder to re-sell the vehicle, leaving you with a disposal liability.

Exercise influence over your community

There are things you can do to influence your condo board or community association. Your condo association might install a larger electrical trunkline to charge electric cars in their parking lot. Your apartment owner might replace all building windows with triple panes to save on heating/cooling costs and reduce street noise. Your community might install solar panels on the community centre to reduce electricity costs and help charge electric cars. You might set up a local community wind and solar power market, behind the transformer. Install a Vanadium Flow Battery (my favourite kind) to store power for times of blackout. Owning local power backup makes your community a more desirable place to live, and your property more valuable. And write, write, write to your government representatives. Governments are only as good as the pressure we put on them.

Is a change of consciousness needed?

Climate change is in my view a symptom of a much-larger problem: the global economy is out of balance with the carrying capacity of the world. Corporations are considered people and are consciously and unconsciously, sacrificing Nature for profit, growth, and shareholder value. What I discussed so far relates to new technologies and redesigning energy systems, moving humanity towards sustainability. That is part of the solution. The other part is "De-Growth"; the need to reduce global consumption and production, which also reduces emissions. Capitalism and global economic growth need a change of intention: a systems-level change, a conscious redesign, and most likely need to shrink in alignment with our unfolding impetus to conserve more energy and want less stuff. Let's explore that.

What if... such change means wealth is not able to concentrate with so few people, regardless of the good they do or don't do with it? What if... the negative damage to Nature and people caused by economic activity were measured and added to the accounting bottom line of all businesses? We call these "negative externalities" because the harm they cause is external to corporate accounting practices and do not affect the business's profitability. An example might be a business that does very good things but also causes pollution which diminishes local property values, hurts people's health, and lowers biodiversity. A carbon tax can curb the negative externality of CO_2 emissions from industrial activity and dissuade people from burning gasoline and diesel to drive their cars. Our economies won't change until our values change. How might we live and what might we value if we factored negative externalities into our own choices? I think this would lead to a change of consciousness. In our current dominant western culture, we revere those few who have reached the top of the financial pyramid. What if ... we no longer aspired to be very rich people and no longer put wealthy people at the top and instead, aspire to an "Elegant Life"?

I define Elegance as the combination of Beauty and Simplicity. We all want meaningful work that provides good food, clean water, health, education, shelter, with enough resiliency to save for our elder years. We want to feel safe at home, in the community and have positive connections with friends and neighbours. We want to have enough time to do satisfying things and contribute to our families and societies. An Elegant Life is a call to being more conscious and grateful regarding one's energy footprints. One might steward all the materials in one's life so that they do not end up in landfills, by donating or fixing things that are no longer needed. Everything goes somewhere. Addressing climate change is both a mandate and an opportunity to build new systems which reduce emissions while re-designing our human systems for the better. The strength that comes from hope is unmatchable. With some hope, luck and effort, our collective work will mean Net Zero by 2050 while also manifesting all 17 of the UN Sustainable Developmental Goals. It means revamping economic systems and instilling a deep love and respect for Nature.

The big finish

To wrap it up... we have *a lot* to do. If we get this right, the future looks attractive. Imagine, Nature and all our relations are thriving. Large habitats are restored and protected on land and in oceans, with a goal of 50 percent protected by 2050. Humans are living sustainably and well within Nature's boundaries. The air is clean. Water is sweet. Cities are safer and quieter. We are comfortable with affordable, reliable clean energy and the cost of all services we rely on has decreased. Everyone has what they need. The population is stable. Companies are doing well financially and work for the good of everybody in the long run. The circular economy is robust. I could go on... and on... and on... but you get my drift. If we get this energy transition right, future generations will look back at us, when we are ancestors, and laugh saying, "I can't believe they burned this valuable hydrocarbon stuff!"

May it be so.

• • •

Maggie Hanna is a geologist with a BSc in Geology with experience in mining, and oil and gas exploration. She currently focuses on systems thinking and energy transition as a Fellow at the Energy Futures Lab, Associate at the Canadian Energy Systems Analysis Research group at the University of Calgary, and Technology Steward with Engineering Change Lab. Her advisory company Common Ground Energy Corp. is stewarding game-changing startup technology companies that provide energy transition advice and develop pathways for established companies to become 'future fit'. Her blog "How the Future Can Go Really, Really Well," highlights daily real-world events that represent evidence of tangible worldwide progress addressing climate change. Maggie lives at the intersection of science and spirit. Her spiritual side is cultivated on the Inayatiyya Sufi Path, and through three decades of friendship and Indigenous learning with her Cree sister Moss Roan of Ermineskin Cree Nation.

NARCISSUS REIMAGINED

Etching on hand-dyed Japanese paper,
Chine-collé, 2020, 48.3 x 33 cm.

Tara Manyfingers

STATEMENT

Narcissus Reimagined exposes the gap between western modern society and indigenous culture. In this current unfolding reality, the balance between the natural ecosystem and "man" has been upset by non-renewable energy extraction. Truth and reconciliation imply the full acknowledgment of the historical actions that brought about climate changes and disparities experienced by the Indigenous Peoples in North America. The annually collected volumetric data from the melting Athabasca Glaciers is as undeniable as the impacts of colonization, and economic activity that shapes how we live and interact today. Therefore, I found it imperative to include natural leaf and feather elements of soft ground etching, entwined with opposing contrasting mythologies. The pathways connecting the highway of tears highlight acts of violence against indigenous communities and the ecosystems of waterways from British

Columbia to Alberta. The highway of tears is embedded in the mountains in this image. The colour of this hand-dyed Chine-Collé image reflects that of a turquoise Lake Louise. It has been documented that this colour comes from the finely ground rock flour contained in the melting icecaps and is disappearing in nature as it is washed away through the Rocky Mountains and settles on the bottom of bodies of water. Essentially Narcissus cannot see beyond himself, and water too is commodified, bottled, and capitalized.

• • •

Tara Manyfingers has varied experience and training ranging from hands-on forklift driving in a warehouse, to handling hazardous materials as a lab technician. She has a Theatre Production Diploma from MacEwan University and worked in several capacities for drafting, set construction, rigging, wardrobe inventory, garment construction, furniture design, lighting, and audio technician in several theatres. She received her Bachelor in Fine Arts at the Alberta University of the Arts in 2019, and is currently pursuing a Master degree of Fine Arts at the Alberta University of the Arts, majoring in printmaking. She is working with Alana Bartol and her thesis work revolves around clean water rights (especially for Indigenous boil water communities).

EPILOGUE

ChatGPT REIMAGINES FIRE

EVELINE KOLIJN ASKS CHATGPT

We will arrive in the future. The arrow of time in which we are situated tells us it will come to pass. How much can we intentionally steer toward our future when it mostly is determined by our combined actions and reactions in our daily lives? In some contributions in this volume, we refer to the increasing application of Artificial Intelligence systems, to help us navigate the complexity of our changing world.

In the months leading to this publication, a public debate started revolving around the astounding development of ChatGPT, an artificial intelligence program, that can answer questions with surprising reasoning and coherence in writing. This version is only the beginning. The big question is what this means for our human capacity to learn and write our own arguments, thinking and research; what it means for creativity and what happens if the written responses are taken as a guide for decisions and actions by the person or institution inputting their query. The ChatGPT voice seems impersonal and apolitical. However, we need not forget this is an algorithm that selects and combines its answers by combing through the internet databases. So, it is not that impersonal: it reflects the most probable, affirmed information relevant to the input query, which has been up to now mostly created through human input. This algorithm certainly has no empathy, ethics, or consciousness. Its answers are devoid of moral judgment, which makes this development a very double-edged sword.

That all being said it may be interesting for the reader to ponder the following "conversation" between myself and ChatGPT-Jan-9-Version which took place on January 18, 2023.

The generated text has not been edited or shortened.

Eveline: How do you reimagine fire?

ChatGPT: Reimagining fire can involve thinking about new ways to harness its energy and power, while also addressing its negative impacts on the environment and human safety.

One way to reimagine fire is to use it as a clean and renewable energy source. For example, biomass-based fire, such as burning wood chips or agricultural waste, can be used to generate electricity in a process called "biomass combustion." This type of fire is considered renewable because the carbon dioxide emitted during combustion is absorbed by new growth in the biomass.

Another way to reimagine fire is to use it in a controlled and safe manner, such as in the form of cooking or heating stoves that are designed to burn fuel more efficiently and emit fewer pollutants. This can have a positive impact on air quality and public health. Another way to use fire is in the form of prescribed fire, which is used as a land management tool, to reduce the risk of wildland fire and to maintain the biodiversity of certain ecosystems. Moreover, Fire could also be reimagined in the form of technology, such as advanced fire suppression systems that use sensors, algorithms, and other technologies to detect and extinguish fires more quickly and effectively.

In summary, reimagining fire can involve thinking about new ways to harness its energy and power, while also addressing its negative impacts on the environment and human safety. It could involve using it as a clean energy source, using it in a controlled and safe manner, using it as a land management tool, and using technology to suppress it.

Eveline: What does the future with renewable energy look like?

ChatGPT: The future with renewable energy is expected to involve a significant increase in the use of clean energy sources such as solar, wind, and hydroelectric power. This shift is likely to lead to a reduction in greenhouse gas emissions, as well as an improvement in air and water quality. Additionally, advances in technology are expected to make renewable energy more cost-effective and efficient, making it increasingly accessible to individuals and businesses. It is also expected that the integration of renewable energy into the grid will become more complex, with the use of smart grids and energy storage becoming more prevalent. Overall, the future with renewable energy is expected to be characterized by a greater emphasis on sustainability and a reduction in dependence on fossil fuels.

Eveline: Should our world shift away from fossil fuels?

ChatGPT: Yes, it is widely recommended that the world should move away from fossil fuels. The burning of fossil fuels such as coal, oil, and natural gas is a major contributor to greenhouse gas emissions and climate change. Climate change poses significant risks to global health, food security, and the economy, and reducing the use of fossil fuels is seen as a crucial step in mitigating these risks.

In addition to the environmental benefits, a shift away from fossil fuels can also have social and economic benefits. Renewable energy sources such as solar and wind power are becoming increasingly affordable and can create new jobs and economic opportunities. Additionally, reducing dependence on fossil fuels can help reduce geopolitical tensions and improve energy security.

It is important to note that a transition away from fossil fuels will not happen overnight and will require significant investment, policy changes, and international cooperation. However, many experts believe that a transition to a low-carbon energy system is necessary and achievable, and that the benefits of such a transition will far outweigh the costs.

Eveline: How should our world decarbonize?

ChatGPT: Decarbonizing the world is a complex and multifaceted process that requires a multi-pronged approach. Here are some of the key strategies that can help achieve this goal:

Increasing the use of renewable energy: This includes promoting the use of solar, wind, hydro, and other renewable energy sources, as well as investing in research and development to make them even more efficient and affordable.

Improving energy efficiency: This involves reducing energy

consumption by improving the energy efficiency of buildings, appliances, and other equipment.

Electrification: This involves increasing the use of electricity as a source of energy, especially in sectors such as transportation, heating and cooling, and industrial processes.

Carbon capture and storage (CCS): This involves capturing carbon dioxide emissions from industrial processes and storing them underground, reducing the amount of carbon dioxide released into the atmosphere.

Promoting sustainable agriculture and forestry practices: This includes reducing deforestation, protecting wetlands and other ecosystems that absorb carbon, and promoting sustainable land-use practices.

Developing low-carbon alternatives: This includes investing in research and development of low-carbon alternatives to fossil fuels, such as biofuels and hydrogen.

Government policy: Governments can play a crucial role in decarbonizing the world by setting targets and policies to reduce greenhouse gas emissions, promoting the use of renewable energy, and supporting low-carbon technologies.

This is by no means an exhaustive list, but it provides a general overview of the main strategies that can help achieve the goal of decarbonizing the world.

Eveline: Can we reach the greenhouse gas targets of the Paris accord?

ChatGPT: Reaching the greenhouse gas reduction targets of the Paris accord, which is to limit global warming to well below 2 degrees Celsius above pre-industrial levels, will require significant effort from governments, businesses, and individuals around the world. The Paris Agreement calls for countries to submit their own voluntary targets for reducing greenhouse gas emissions, known as Nationally Determined Contributions (NDCs)

However, as of today, current NDCs submitted by countries are not enough to reach the target of keeping the temperature increase below 2C, the target set in the Paris Agreement. According to the United Nations Framework Convention on Climate Change (UNFCCC) and other independent analysis, to limit warming to 2C, global emissions must decline by around 45% from 2010 levels by 2030 and reach net-zero by around 2050.

Achieving these targets will require a significant reduction in emissions from the energy sector, particularly in the use of fossil fuels such as coal, oil, and natural gas. This will require a shift to clean energy sources such as wind, solar, and hydroelectric power, as well as investment in energy efficiency and conservation measures. Additionally, it will require a reduction in emissions from other sectors such as transportation, agriculture, and industry, through the use of low-carbon technologies and practices.

In summary, reaching the greenhouse gas reduction targets of the Paris accord is possible, but it will require a significant and concerted effort from all sectors of society, including government, business, and individuals, as well as a strong international cooperation.

Eveline: A small population has little impact on global emissions. Will it make a difference if they put effort in decarbonizing society?

ChatGPT: It is true that a small population has a relatively small impact on global greenhouse gas emissions when compared to larger populations or major emitters such as China and the United States. However, every effort to reduce emissions can contribute to the global effort to combat climate change, and it is important to remember that the Paris agreement is based on the principle of "common but differentiated responsibility" which means that all countries should contribute to the effort according to their own capabilities.

Additionally, decarbonizing a society can have a number of other benefits, such as improving air and water quality, reducing dependence on fossil fuels, and creating new jobs and economic opportunities in the clean energy sector. Furthermore, by taking action, small population can set an example for other countries and communities, encouraging them to take similar steps towards decarbonization.

It's also worth noting that, even if a small population's impact on global emissions is small, it can still be affected by climate change, so it's important to take action to mitigate the effects of climate change.

In conclusion, while small populations may have a relatively small impact on global greenhouse gas emissions, it is still important for them to take action to reduce their emissions and to contribute to the global effort to combat climate change. The effort put into decarbonizing their society will make a difference on their own community, and can also set an example for others to follow.

Eveline: How will energy transition impact biodiversity on the planet?

ChatGPT: The energy transition, or the shift from fossil fuels to renewable energy sources, has the potential to both positively and negatively impact biodiversity on the planet.

On the positive side, the increased use of renewable energy sources such as solar and wind power can help to reduce greenhouse gas emissions, which are a major driver of climate change. Climate change is a major threat to biodiversity and by reducing emissions, the energy transition can help to mitigate this threat. Furthermore, the transition to renewable energy can also help to reduce air and water pollution, which can also have a positive impact on biodiversity.

On the negative side, the energy transition can also have negative impacts on biodiversity. For example, the construction of large-scale renewable energy projects such as wind farms or hydroelectric dams can have negative impacts on wildlife, habitats and ecosystems. It's also important to consider the impacts of the construction and materials used in the development of renewable energy projects.

In conclusion, the energy transition has the potential to both positively and negatively impact biodiversity on the planet. It is important to consider the potential impacts of renewable energy projects on biodiversity and to minimize negative impacts through careful planning, location selection and management. Additionally, it's important to remember that the shift to renewable energy is necessary to mitigate the effects of climate change on biodiversity.

ACKNOWLEDGEMENTS

Eveline Kolijn

THIS BOOK has been conceived, created and produced in Alberta, the traditional land of many Indigenous Peoples, presently subject to Treaty 6, Treaty 7, and Treaty 8. These are the Blackfoot Confederacy—Kainai, Piikani, and Siksika—the Cree, Dene, Saulteaux, Nakota Sioux, Stoney Nakoda, and the Tsuut'ina Nation, and the Métis People of Alberta. This includes the Métis Settlements and the Six Regions of the Métis Nation of Alberta within the historical Northwest Métis Homeland. In view of the future changes that are coming, I want to acknowledge the many Peoples who have lived on and cared for these lands for generations. I am grateful for the traditional Knowledge Keepers and Elders who are still with us today and those who continue teaching us their knowledge and respect for the land.

This publication has evolved from the Energy Futures print-portfolio project, which I conceived of and produced with generous assistance and funding from the Energy Futures Lab's Impact Studio initiative. I would like to thank Managing Director Alison Cretney for greenlighting my project, and Emily Blocksom, Emma Gammans and Kelley Thompson for all their feedback in developing the proposal and assistance in organizing and recording the large Zoom sessions with all participants. The support from the Energy Futures Lab contributed to securing additional funding from the Alberta Foundation for the Arts and Calgary Arts Development.

Many thanks to the Fellows from the Energy Futures Lab, who presented in Zoom sessions, to inform the artists and authors on several aspects and technologies in the energy transition in Alberta: Yasmin Abram, Diandra Bruised Head, Marie Golonka, Terri-Lynn Duque, Maggie Hanna, Liz Lappin, Megan Lohman, Gary Millard, Candice Paton, Luisa da Silva, and Alison Thompson. As well as these Fellows, who made themselves available and provided in-person information and feedback: Matt Beck, Liz Brennan, James van Leeuwen, Petr Musilek, Brad Nickel, and Binnu Yeyakumar.

To all the artists and authors who responded to the call for participation and became part of this project, thank you. You gave this book an incredible and inspiring variety of contributions. Some of you assisted with extra tasks, such as writing letters of recommendation, collecting the print editions, or editing: Lori Claerhout, Barb Howard, Jill Ho-You, Alice Major and Richard Harrison, who gave substantial input on the Introduction. Nadia Perna created a beautiful cover design. My sincere thanks to Chris Turner for adding his voice and writing a wonderful foreword to this volume.

Many thanks to my fantastic publisher, Lorene Shyba, from the small but mighty indie press: Durvile & UpRoute Books. Lorene has embraced this book with great energy and enthusiasm from the beginning. She has expertly guided me in evolving this book and has put a lot of effort into producing a good-looking publication and managing its distribution. Without her, this book would not exist. Thanks also to Cole Girodat and Julian Hobson for proofreading.

Finally, for his unwavering support and for helping to keep my life going while I was busy with this project, love and thanks to my life partner and husband Cornelis.

IMAGE CREDITS

All photos by Eveline Kolijn

Except:

Sylvia Arthur, pages 14, 22.

Jared Tailfeathers, pages 24, 40.

Kasia Koralewska, page 48.

Jamie-Lee Girodat, pages 50, 54.

Mary Kavanagh, page x, 64, 80.

Nadia Perna, pages 84, 96.

Kate Baillies, pages 98.

Heather Urness, 134.

Hannah Gelderman, page 144.

Stan Phelps, page 166.

Liz Ingram, pages 214, 228.

ENVIRONMENTAL
SUSTAINABILITY

To reflect the theme of the book on its manufacture, care has been taken to select the paper and inks from sustainable and low-carbon impact sources.

The book was printed by Friesens Press in single-colour runs with vegetable-based inks. The pages are printed on 100 percent recycled, FSC-certified, uncoated Enviro white. The cover is printed on Milkweed card stock manufactured by Mohawk Loop. Mohawk Loop is a comprehensive collection of high post-consumer waste (PCW) recycled papers to support sustainable design.

Plastic lamination on paperback books render them non-biodegradable, so in an effort to limit our plastic waste, the jacket cover is not laminated. Please handle the book with care.

ENVIRONMENTAL BENEFITS STATEMENT

Durvile Publications Ltd saved the following resources by printing the pages of this book on chlorine free paper made with 100% post-consumer waste.

TREES	WATER	ENERGY	SOLID WASTE	GREENHOUSE GASES
5 FULLY GROWN	**1630** *LITRES*	**2.1** *GIGAJOULES*	**8.2** *KILOGRAMS*	**1,000** *KILOGRAMS*

Environmental impact estimates were made using the Environmental Paper Network Paper Calculator 4.0. *and converted to Metric Measures.*

ABOUT THE EDITOR
EVELINE KOLIJN

Eveline Kolijn is a printmaker and installation artist living and working in Calgary, Alberta, Canada. She spent her childhood beachcombing the shores of Venezuela and in her teens, scuba diving in the Caribbean. These experiences influenced her development as an artist and interest in the connections between art, science, environmental awareness, and climate change. Eveline received a MA in cultural anthropology from Leiden University in the Netherlands in 1986 and a BFA from the Alberta College of Art+ Design in 2008, including the Governor General's Award for academic achievement. She has participated in national and international exhibitions and residencies, public art projects and community engagement. She has been published in various scientific publications. In 2019, she received the AUArts Alumni Legacy award. In 2022, she created her first full-length film "Winterreise – A Winter's Journey" in collaboration with the Mountainview Festival of Song and Chamber Music. She joined Alberta's Energy Futures Lab as a Fellow in 2018 and has moved on to be an Ambassador for the Lab. She is using the arts and her Fellowship experience to promote energy literacy, awareness, and discussion on a just energy transition.